The National

Donal O'Sullivan has been a member of the National Yacht Club since 1967 and Hon. Sec. of Dublin Bay Sailing Club for 27 years. He is also the author of *Dublin Bay: A Century of Sailing* and *Ó Kingstown go Dún Laoghaire* (Foilseacháin Náisuúnta Teo, 1976).

THE NATIONAL

Chronicles of a
Dún Laoghaire Yacht Club

Donal O'Sullivan

The Liffey Press

Published by
The Liffey Press Ltd
'Clareville'
307 Clontarf Road
Dublin D03 PO46, Ireland
www.theliffeypress.com

A catalogue record of this book is
available from the British Library.

ISBN 978-1-9160998-6-9

Printed in Spain by GraphyCems.

Contents

SIDELINES

ADDENDA

Bourke Builders Ltd – Members and Supporters of the National Yacht Club

Bourke Buliders Ltd (https://bourkebuilders.com) have generously supported the publication of *The National: Chronicles of a Dún Laoghaire Yacht Club* by Donal O'Sullivan. It is a fitting support as the firm, established in Ballina, County Mayo, in 1960, has just completed the superb redevelopment of the building where it all started – Anglesey House, Crofton Road, Dún Laoghaire.

Anglesey House

NYC Member and firm Director Brian Bourke won the club's *Muglin's Cup* for the most interesting family cruise in 2019. He sailed his Oceanis 35 *Zoe B* to St. Kilda, far west of Scotland, last year.

Among the firms' recent projects was the re-development of the former Anglesey Arms Hotel which, as this work reminds us, had its own place in the history of the National Yacht Club. It was in this building, on 26 November 1869, that the club, known originally as the Kingstown Harbour Boat Club, held its inaugural meeting. Its first (joint) Hon. Secretary was Francis Lucas Cadwallader Walshe, who in 1859 had married Maria Rathbone, whose family then owned the hotel.

The following year, on 20 April 1870, after the Earl of Longford had laid the first stone, *The Irish Times* reported: 'The members of the club, with a few friends, adjourned to the Anglesey Arms Hotel, where they enjoyed a dinner fit for a prince. The usual loyal toasts having been proposed and responded to, the future of the club received with cheers, the party separated, having spent a most agreeable evening.'

So initiating, we have no hesitation in observing the tradition of excellent dining with which the club has always been noted!

Bight of the East Pier is host to many NYC boats

Acknowledgements

Many people have helped in the production of this book or contributed in various ways. Their names are listed below. If I have forgotten someone who should be included and is not, my humblest apologies. Needless to add, any error or omissions that may have occurred are mine only.

Roger Bannon, Stephen and Ron Barrington, Rosemary Beckett, Ronan Beirne, Dr. Bernard Bolger, Jeff Brownlee, Frank Burgess, Lucy Burke, Paddy Carmody, Richella Carroll, Captain Simon Coate, Ned Cummins, Fionán de Barra, Oonagh Deegan, Vincent Delany, Peter Gray, Dr. Frank Hegarty, Marcus Higgins, Bernie Hooper, Richard Hooper, Ida Kiernan, Cathy MacAleavey, Martin McCarthy, Barbara McHenry, Barry McNeaney, Justin Merrigan, Chris Moore, Jack Murray, Con Murphy, Sean Nolan, Dan O'Connor, Michael O'Leary, Michael O'Rahilly, Brendan and Conor O'Regan, Barry O'Sullivan, Bairbre O'Sullivan, Michael Rothschild, Nerys and Ken Ryan, John Simington, Ken Slattery and Carmel Winkelmann.

I am particularly indebted to the staffs of the various libraries and archival bodies who have helped with my researches. In particular I thank Nigel Curtin, Local Studies Librarian, Dún Laoghaire Rathdown County Council Library Service, who was very generous with advice on useful sources of enquiry. Brian Donnelly of the National Archives was similarly helpful. I thank, too, the archivist of the Royal College of Surgeons as well as the archival service of the Freemasons, who were most obliging with information on some of the club's founder members.

Also the Officers and secretarial staff of the Royal Irish Yacht Club and the Royal St. George Yacht Club who kindly allowed me to consult their club minutes or letter books. I would also like to mention Hal Sisk who, despite the many demands of his own projects, was most generous with his time and encouragement, particularly in the early stages of the project.

Finally, our warmest thanks to our editorial and production adviser, David Givens of The Liffey Press, for preparing this work for publication.

Donal O'Sullivan
August 2020

Foreword

This year of 2020 marks the 150th year of the presence in this location, beside the East Pier in Dun Laoghaire, of the Sailing Clubhouse of what is now the National Yacht Club.

When the foundation stone was laid by the Earl of Longford on 20 April 1870, Ireland was an incredibly different place to the nation of today, whose national symbol, the harp, we are very proud to share.

The first 60 years of the club's life were exceptionally difficult with wars, civil strife and other factors causing financial and other problems, leading to several liquidations, reconstitutions and renamings of the club.

Martin McCarthy

The election of the Earl of Granard as Commodore in 1931, and the assumption of the new name, 'The National Yacht Club', starts the modern era of the club, which has continued under generally the same constitution and rules for the last 90 years.

It is amazing how well the clubhouse itself, a fine, cut stone building, has adapted to meet the changing requirements of the sailing membership, thanks to the input of many member engineers and architects over the years.

Equally, as temporary custodians of the club, this history reminds us of how the many previous Commodores, Flag Officers and members adapted their policies and operations to meet the ever-changing requirements of Dublin and Ireland's sailing fraternity.

We owe a great debt of gratitude to Donal O'Sullivan who was in a unique position to write this anthology, having been a member of the National Yacht Club since 1967 and Hon. Sec. of Dublin Bay Sailing Club for 27 years, and the author of *Dublin Bay: A Century of Sailing* to celebrate DBSC's 100th in 1984. Donal has an engaging and entertaining writing style with a breathtaking knowledge of who, what, where and when, which captures many of the milestones on the lifetime of the club in the last 150 years.

Today we are especially conscious that the club's good health is due to the great work of previous generations. We are conscious that we are exceptionally fortunate to have an amazingly loyal membership, with some families being involved for three or more generations. The names Murphy, Horgan, Ryan, Roy, Winkelmann, Lemass, Cooney, Byrne, Hall, Shanahan, Gorman, Johnson, Kirwans and others come to mind. The modern generation are every bit as good as their forefathers in undertaking voluntary service for the club.

In 2018, the Dún Laoghaire Rathdown County Council took over the operation of the harbour itself and this has enabled the continuation of a warm and productive relationship between us that stretches back decades, which was highlighted by the jointly organized homecoming to celebrate Annalise Murphy's Olympic Silver medal at the Rio 2016 games – the greatest night in the club's history.

We also thank our neighbouring clubs in the Harbour – DMYC, RIYC and RSGYC – our sister sailing clubs around Ireland and Sailing Ireland, as well as DBSC, ICC, INSS, ISORA and others whose input to the National Yacht Club is generously given and warmly appreciated.

Sailing is a tremendously rewarding sport within which one learns about teamwork, safety, engineering, navigation, interdependence, independence – as well as logistics, finance, fun and sociality.

In Dún Laoghaire we are incredibly privileged to have a fantastic harbour and bay on our doorstep – and that previous generations conceived and built the National Yacht Club that we know and love today.

I hope this volume will enrich your knowledge and understanding of the club, its people and the wider community and supporters.

Martin McCarthy
Commodore

2019/2020 Main Committee of National Yacht Club
(Back row, L-R): John McNeilly, Peter Doran, Clodagh Nolan, Alan Turner, Peter Sherry
Front row (L-R): Michéle Halpenny, Chris Doorly, Martin McCarthy,
Conor O'Regan, Rosemary Cadogen
Co-opted later: William Byrne and Nicole Hemeryke.
(photo: Frank Burgess)

In memory of my dear wife Maureen, who, with perfect good humour, put up with her husband's sailing activities for over 53 years.

1.

Introduction

For now we see through a glass, darkly; but then face to face: now I know in part; but then shall I know even as also I am known.
– St. Paul 1. Corinthians Chap 13 verse 1.

Some civilisations or empires have what is called a Dark Age, variously defined as a deficiency of rational activity over a given period or a simple paucity of record. Coming down from that august level, and leaving rationality aside, we might say that the club that eventually became the National Yacht Club has had its own Dark Age. It extends over the first thirty years of its existence, roughly

1

between the laying of the first stone in April 1870 and the transfer of its assets to the newly-formed Edward Yacht Club in 1901. For this there is virtually no club record whatever. Any that existed would have been destroyed in the two disastrous fires that ravaged the club premises in 1975 and 1984.

Darkness does not have to be totally opaque and, somewhat to my surprise, the mists surrounding the Club's history, when I really set about it and with some diligent digging and delving, proved not be too impenetrable. This is due in no small way to the new online research tools which have made searching through records of the last and previous century so much easier. No more poring over pages and pages of dusty newsprint in the National Library nor searching through sometimes indecipherable baptismal records in dim church vestries.

True, some things never change. When I told someone in the Registry of Deeds that I had been there forty years previously, I was told, 'We haven't changed *that* much, you know.' True enough, except that over the years the ledgers seemed to have become much heavier and I would never have been able to lift some of them were it not for the help of my friend Hal Sisk, who was my stimulating companion during many forays into the club's past.

Delve into the club's history for long enough and after a while you feel that some of the persons you are reading about become like friends or at least people you know very well. Certainly, I would like to have known William le Fanu, the Board of Works commissioner in charge of harbours. He was the official who – I'm quite sure of it – would have given the initial okay to build the clubhouse on Harbour property; clearly a most congenial man, who liked to sit up carousing with friends until the small hours, drinking claret, singing songs and telling stories.

Also Charles Barrington, who climbed the Eiger, rather as an afterthought, and despite what was probably an onerous day-job also looked after three clubs. Indefatigable, he accompanied the Irish cricket team that played in America in 1879 and also *followed* (I think that is the correct term) the Ward Union. His brother, Sir John

Barrington, certainly, who was twice Dublin's Lord Mayor and who laughed at his own pretensions in mock-scriptural verse.

I am not sure about Captain Peter Leslie Peacocke. Here I should register a proviso. The odd reports we have show him as a difficult, argumentative man. The picture could be incomplete; the reality might be different as, indeed, it might be of others in the story. If more information from those times were to turn up, Captain Peacocke might be shown to be one of those unfortunate persons whom things just happen to. So, a caveat: of necessity the picture we have of him and the others could be partial; it is based on pieces of information that just happen to have come to light.

A couple of necessary footnotes. This work seeks to build up a picture of the club's history, not of physical or organisational structures – the lack of most of the club's records precludes that – but with the stories of the people who featured or who contributed to it in some way. It's so easy to get lost among the interesting side issues one has to follow-up to get at some semblance of the real story.

Some of them are fascinating but to include them in the main narrative would complicate the story line. And yet they can form a background against which things happened and it would be pity if they were overlooked or lost to common memory. So they have been included at the end in a separate section. I've refrained from calling it appendices –it's not that kind of book – but instead entitled them Sidelines because that in fact is what they are.

I have called the work Chronicles – not a history – of a Dún Laoghaire Yacht Club. A yacht club, a building, is not something you can easily put a history on, not least this one, which, as mentioned, lost over a hundred years of its records in two disastrous conflagrations. So what is presented here is a narrative of the club's evolution with particular reference to the people who featured in the club's story, or who gave the club a certain quality which some are inclined to think characteristic of the National Yacht Club.

The Greek word *ethos* would be too grand to describe it. Rather, it's a certain singularity, a disinclination to be too predictable or over-respectful to convention or the accepted way of doing things.

The sainted Cardinal Newman, in describing a certain authority of outlook derived from residence at an Oxford or Cambridge college, used the Latin phrase *genius loci*, the spirit of the place, so to speak. We for our part might think of one of the ancient gods of these parts, Manannán Mac Lir, who went around in disguise, playing tricks, performing wonders and generally stirring things up.

Finally, the name of the place where a lot of what is recorded here occurred. All, or a sizable majority of the inhabitants at the time, were totally different to ourselves in political outlook and social attitude. Drinking the Queen's health at their functions happened automatically. Some, or perhaps members of their families, served Queen and Country overseas in distant parts of the Empire. They had no trouble in calling the place where they lived Kingstown and it seems natural to continue to do so here until a big upheaval in the township was recorded in 1920.

That happened at a meeting, on 6 July, of the Kingstown Town Council. A motion, proposed by Councillor Sean Ó hUadhaigh and supported by a majority of the councillors was passed that replaced the name Kingstown with the historic one of Dún Laoghaire.

Years later, at some Irish language event, I met the actual proposer of that motion in his old age. I remember thinking at the time that he didn't look like a revolutionary; rather, he seemed like a gracious gentleman from earlier times, with the gentle humour and the fine manners of a Kingstown solicitor. Politics had changed but the people, it seemed, not that much.

Donal O'Sullivan
July 2020

2.

Arte et Animo
(Skill and Courage)

'... a chastely engraved silver trowel, manufactured by Mr. Brunker, of Grafton St., Dublin, was presented to Lord Longford by one of the honorary secretaries, Captain F L C Walshe. The trowel was worthy of the occasion, being surmounted by the motto of the club, arte et animo.'

The long, eventful, story of the National Yacht Club begins on a beautiful spring afternoon in 1870. On 20 April of that year, a body of local notables, watched by a crowd of curious onlookers, gathered on a space between the Carlisle and the East Piers to witness the laying of the foundation stone of what was first styled the Kingstown Royal Harbour Boat Club. The ceremony was performed by the Earl of Longford, **owner of extensive property in county Dublin, not least in Kingstown and the counties of Westmeath and Longford.**

Kingstown of those years was an attractive and tranquil Anglo-Irish enclave, hardly, if at all, affected by the Fenian Rising which had shaken other parts of the country a bare three years before. It was a sunny, late spring day. The sailing season – or what passed for such at the time – had hardly commenced, but already in the harbour were a number of yachts at anchor.

Many were of a considerable tonnage, much heavier than you would see today in the locality: Jameson's *Gitana* weighed 75 tons; John Kelly's *Vision*, 52 tons; R.N. Batt's, *Zema*, 52 tons; George Putland's *Enid*, 57 tons. The schooner, *Halcyon*, belonging to J. McAuliffe, weighed 40 tons. Smaller craft were a minority. It would be another fourteen years before Dublin Bay Sailing Club came on the scene to provide for more modest craft – those of twenty-one feet and under. And for owners with more modest incomes.

Near where the East pier joins the Kingstown shore, between the East and the Carlisle piers, Mr. Cunningham, 'the well-known and eminent contractor' (so described by *The Irish Times*), had erected a commodious viewing platform. It was built to accommodate an assembly of ladies, 'fair and beautiful', who had come to view the ceremony. Another platform accommodated the male guests and promotors of the project: James Milo Bourke, chairman of the Dalkey Commissioners and universally known as the Father of Dalkey; Captain Hutchison, RN (Harbour Master); Captain F.L.C. Walshe; W. Beatty; H. Scott; W. Scott; W. Murphy; John Dennehy; John Crowe; W.A Emerson; A. Findlater; Pierce Stevens, the architect for the building; William Stirling; and Dr. Falkner among others.

Also on the platform was a pair of shears supporting the foundation stone. This was a type of derrick, three poles joined together in a sort of A frame with a block and tackle. It was commonly used for lifting weights before the forklift truck came into use. The next day's issue of *Saunders Newsletter* carried a description of the proceedings:

> The foundation stone of this Club was laid -- by the Rt. Hon. The Earl of Longford. 'At about half past five the stone was lowered, a bottle containing the coins in circulation, wrapped

in copies of *Saunders Newsletter*, *Freeman's Journal* and *The Irish Times* being first deposited in the cavity underneath. Lord Longford was then handed a very handsome silver trowel which bore an inscription to the effect that 'the first stone of the Royal Harbour Boat Club was laid by the Hon. Major General the Earl of Longford'.

This nobleman, then having completed the laying of the stone, declared it well and truly laid. Afterwards, his lordship said he thanked them for the honour they had that day conferred on him; that he hoped the club would prosper and alluded to 'yachtsman exercising their muscles as well as their brains'. Cheers were then given for the noble lord and the success of the club, after which the assembly separated.

The Irish Times report had some further details of the ceremony:

About 5 o'clock a chastely engraved silver trowel, manufactured by Mr. Brunker, of Grafton St., Dublin, was presented to Lord Longford by one of the honorary secretaries, Captain F L C Walshe. The trowel was worthy of the occasion, being surmounted by the motto of the club, *arte et animo*, and bore the following inscription: 'presented to the Major General the Right Hon the Earl of Longford, KCB, on the occasion of his laying the first stone of the Kingstown Royal Harbour Boat Club, on the 20th April 1870.

Saunders reported that after the ceremony the assembly separated. Not quite. Perhaps *The Irish Times* correspondent had better contacts (this was probably the Mr W.A. Emerson, mentioned above). He was able to report:

Three cheers were then given for the laying of the stone, another three for the Noble Mason, Lord Longford, after which the members of the club, with a few friends, adjourned to the Anglesey Arms Hotel, where they enjoyed a dinner fit for a prince. The usual loyal toasts having been proposed and responded to, and the future of the club received with cheers, the party separated, having spent a most agreeable evening.

The noble lord who laid the foundation stone was the 4th Earl. He succeeded, in 1860, his brother the 3rd Earl of whom Maria Edgeworth wrote:

> He is an amiable-looking youth – I should guess on much talent – in the guards – and does not love drinking or gambling – and if she (his mother) gives him his head may run his course well.

Misjudged optimism, according to Valerie Pakenham, who edited Edgeworth's letters, 'the 3rd Earl was to die in unsavoury circumstances in London aged forty-three.'

The 4th Earl had sterner qualities. Having entered the army in 1837, he served in the Crimea and the Indian rebellion, becoming Adjutant-General in India in 1858. In the House of Lords he served as Under-Secretary for War during the administrations of Earl of Derby and Benjamin Disraeli. Another position which he held (following the disestablishment of the Church of Ireland in 1869) was chairman of the Protestant Defence League. Before the Land League agitation, according to his obituary, he was one of the most popular landlords in the county, being a resident on his property, who expended a large sum in local improvements and gave extensive employment.

The stone-laying ceremony was the formal launching of the club but to make it all happen much work had to go on beforehand. Most conveniently, a reporter from the *Freeman's Journal* was on hand in the Anglesey Arms Hotel, Kingstown on 26 November 1869 to report on the club's inaugural meeting. It's worth reading to get a sense of the enthusiasm that inspired its founding fathers, as well as the clear statement of purposes that the club was intended to serve.

Kingstown Harbour Boat Club

A meeting of the most influential residents of Kingstown and its neighbourhood was held on Friday evening in the Anglesey Arms Hotel, Kingstown, for the purpose of taking measures for the formation and management of a rowing club which will bear the above name. Amongst those present were:-

John Crosthwaite,TC; Dr.O'Flaherty, F.W. Murray, F.A.. Doyle, C E, Taylor, R.C. Lee, Blackrock: Myles Kelly, TC, J. Browne, Walter Fitzsimons, John Holland, Harry Scott, P. Lagan, TC, J.M. Inglis, P. Hayes, S. Creagh, jnr., Colville Jones, Geo. Smith, R.J. Ennis, John H. Samuels, Joseph Beatty, John Lalor, Wm.Sterling, CE; J. Ratigan, S.B. Bowles, R. Molloy, F. Whelan, G.S.B. Sinclair, B.M. Sinclair, FLC Walshe, Simon Creagh, Richard O'Flaherty, W.P. Weldon, W.R. Beatty.

On the motion of Mr. Simon Creagh, seconded by Mr. Colville Jones, the chair was taken, amid applause, by John J. Crosthwaite, Esq., TC.

The chairman thus addressed the meeting:-

Gentlemen, I thank you heartily for having done me the honour of asking me to preside on this occasion. When I look around me, and see this assemblage of wealth and rank which is joining in this, our undertaking , I feel that, though it is small at present, yet we have the germ of its success in this room, (applause); and I believe that when we have formed the club, and when our men and boats have had a due amount of practice, Kingstown Harbour will be fully able to compete, in point of rowing skill, with any seaport town in the United Kingdom, and probably in America (loud applause).

There were some gentlemen from America last season, and I should have liked to have seen them on the waters of Kingstown (hear, hear). So anxious was I that we should compete with them here, that I offered to entertain them, and I also offered a hundred guinea prize for competition. But I was told they could not come. However, we have it yet in store for them (laughter) and I think we should hold out every inducement for them to come here. I am satisfied that that if they do come, we will not allow them to take the prize out of Kingstown (applause).

Mr. W.B. Beatty was appointed secretary to the meeting, on the motion of Mr. A. Samuels, seconded by Mr. FLC Walshe.

Dr. O'Flaherty then proposed and Mr. Murray seconded a resolution to the effect – 'That a club, to be called the Kingstown Harbour Boat Club, be and is hereby formed.' The resolution was put and carried.

Mr. George Smith proposed 'That the annual subscription to the club be two guineas, and that the members be admitted by ballot.' Mr. John H. Samuels seconded the resolution, which passed.

A resolution was then proposed by Mr. Fitzsimons, seconded by Mr. Taylor, and carried, submitting to the meeting the names of those gentlemen who had been selected to form a temporary committee.

Some discussion having taken place on this subject, Messrs. F.L.C. Walshe, W.B. Beatty and James Beatty were formally appointed honorary officers and *ex-officio* members of the committee, the first and second as secretaries and the last as treasurer.

A subscription list was opened after the transaction of the above business, and almost all the gentlemen present placed their names on it for subscriptions of various sums. Mr. Crosthwaite announced his intention, amid loud and prolonged applause, to give £50 to the club, and headed the list with his name for that amount.

The second chair was taken by Dr. O'Flaherty. Mr. Kelly then proposed a vote of thanks to Mr. Crosthwaite. Mr. Walshe seconded the motion, and in doing so, said that Mr. Crosthwaite had proved himself worthy of being called 'the Peabody of Kingstown'. (Hear, hear).

Mr. Sterling, C.E., having been admitted as life-member free, in return for his professional services, to be gratuitously given by him at the building of the new club-house.

The meeting separated.....................

The club, then, was established to serve people whose recreation was rowing boats. It was to be a rowing club without any ostensible or understated ambition to develop into a yacht club. It was not set up in opposition to the existing two royal yacht clubs. Nor is there any suggestion that it would be there to accommodate any particular section or cohort of the local community. Not for the landed gentry, or people associated with them, nor for people 'in trade' who felt excluded from the Royal St. George Yacht Club, nor for people of a Catholic persuasion who might have felt uncomfortable in the other clubs (though with little reason to, it's been pointed out, particularly in the case of the Royal Irish since one of its founders included John O'Connell, son of the Liberator).

In fact, any suggestion that the new club was set up by Catholics unhappy with their reception elsewhere can be dismissed out of the hand. Indeed, all or most of the club's founders were of Church of Ireland affiliation – and Freemasons at that. Nothing odd about that either. At that time, and in that area, for people in business or the professions, membership of a lodge was normal; it brought useful friendships and provided an outlet for charitable inclinations consistent with the high moral tone of the period.

One of the first Hon. Secretaries was not a mason but very probably Church of Ireland. His full name was Francis Lucas Cadwallader Walshe. He married, on 18 May 1859 in St. Marks Parish Church (Church of Ireland) Maria Rathbone, one of the Rathbone family who at the time owned the Anglesey Arms Hotel. Interestingly, in *Thom's Directory* of 1872, Francis had become the owner of the hotel. In *The Irish Times* report on the stone-laying ceremony he was described as Captain F.L.C. Walshe, but this rank was not repeated later in directory entries.

His father's occupation on the marriage certificate was given as 'gentleman', as was that of the bride's father. Another early member, Deane Shelton, was a son of Grantley Shelton, a Church of Ireland clergyman from Charleville, County Cork. When he married Emma Ann Atkinson in 1882 both their religious denominations were described on the marriage certificate as Church of Ireland.

Another of the promotors of the new club was Thomas Brunker, whose business address was 111 Grafton Street. *Thom's Directory* of 1871 described him as a jeweller and manufacturer of masonic ornaments and Paris clocks. The masonic connection would suggest that he, too, was Protestant.

Portrait of John Crosthwaite

And what of John Crosthwaite, Town Councillor, who made that stirring introductory address and who in putting up £50 showed he was putting his money where his mouth was? He was undoubtedly a Catholic; he contributed £45 to the St. Michael's Hospital building fund and in 1876 was a member of a Catholic union set up by the hierarchy to support the Pope and the Church on the continent from anti-clerical attacks.

His very interesting portrait, with high forehead and dark intelligent eyes, would suggest a man of intellectual interests rather than someone from the commercial world. His legacy as a builder has to be Crosthwaite Park, which he developed in the 1860s in the form of a square with handsome houses on two sides. Undoubtedly he was endowed with considerable public spirit, attending 174 meetings of the Kingstown Commissioners in 1874. He served *eight* times as chairman of the Commissioners and was occupying that role when he died in 1884 in his ninetieth year.

He was no pushover in an argument. When the Board of the Commissioners were awarding the contract for the sewage works for the Kingstown and Glasthule wards to someone who seems to have been a relation of one of their own members, he made his disapproval very plain. In his view, Mr John Cunningham, whose tender was just £2 higher than the winner's, should have been awarded the contract. (This was John Cunningham the 'well-known and eminent contractor', who earlier had built the Kingstown Royal Harbour Boat Club.) The *Freeman* reported: 'Mr.Crosthwaite arose and speaking in an excited manner, said there was never a more unjust act about to be perpetrated. After some further observations, Mr. Crosthwaite left the room, charging the Board with dishonesty.'

Yet for all the solid business acumen of the founding fathers, and the enthusiastic pledges of support at the first meeting, there was an odd lack of curiosity about the dimensions of the clubhouse they were contributing to. Yachting at the time enjoyed enormous societal éclat and the social life associated with it required clubhouses of a certain size. Could the same be said about rowing? True enough, its public profile at the time was much greater than it is now, but would the actual scale of the activity merit a clubhouse in Kingstown that in today's money was to cost the best part of four million euro?

One thing is certain, and that motion of George Smith's at the first meeting provides a useful indication – members would be admitted by ballot. In other words, the club was going to be a gentleman's club like any other, with all the expected amenities including dining facilities, a billiard room, a bar, a cardroom and so on.

And, of course, an acceptable standard of behaviour …

3.

A Problem and a Solution

It's curious how the promoters of the new club managed so easily to get the permission of the Commissioners of Public Works (*ex-officio*, Commissioners of Kingstown Harbour) to build on this site. It was by no means a simple matter. In fact, thirty years earlier, when promoters of the Royal Irish Yacht Club sought permission to build their clubhouse, they had run into a considerable bureaucratic quagmire.

The RIYC, at the time, had had the Queen as patron, the Marquess of Donegall as its Commodore and sundry cross-channel worthies as honorary members. Yet, for all this weighty patronage, the promotors suffered serious cross-fire from a combination of Lords of the Treasury, the Lords of the Admiralty and the Commissioners of Public works; all of whom believed they had an unalienable right to be heard on all matters pertaining to the Royal Asylum Harbour.

The Treasury Under-Secretary at the time was the formidable Charles Edward Trevelyan; his malign memory is still evoked whenever Irish rugby supporters sing *The Fields of Athenry*. Some modern historians defend Trevelyan and his famine policy on the grounds that he was merely the helpless and low-level executor of the economic doctrine of the time. But one of Trevelyan's utterances will never be easily forgotten on this side the Channel: 'The greatest evil we have to face is not the physical evil of the famine but the moral evil of the selfish, perverse and turbulent character of the Irish people.'

You can get a flavour of the unbending Trevelyan mindset in one of his letters in a National Archive file relative to the building of the Royal Irish clubhouse:

> Since their Lordships were first called upon to interfere for the protection of the public interest in connection with this subject-------- it was incumbent on them not to allow any portion of this last mentioned piece of land to be permanently alienated except on such conditions as would prevent any plan which may hereafter be resolved upon for laying it out for the public advantage being interfered with.

With the memory of all this bureaucratic obstructionism still very much alive – as was Trevelyan himself, though far away in India – the wonder has to be that the proposers of the new club managed to get their project accepted with such surprising ease. The RSGYC, for their part, had been able to circumvent any objection with a bit of harmless subterfuge – they had described the structure as a simple boathouse. This gave the Board of Works the impression that what was in mind was much more modest than what finally emerged, namely, a 'lofty club-house'. They were very cross about it – or certainly gave that impression.

As it happens, the two situations are different in one respect. The Board of Works were inded willing to give the Royal Irish a site for their clubhouse, but not where they wanted. Hence the appeal to Whitehall and the involvement of Trevelyan et al. This does not seem to have been an issue with the site of the Kingstown Boat Club (now the NYC).

It was fortunate that the Commissioners of Public Works in Ireland at the time were very notable public servants, well capable of making up their own minds as to where the public interest lay. The most eminent of them was Sir Richard Griffith, better known today as the author of the Griffith Valuation, still an invaluable source for local and genealogical studies; it is said that he was bossy and demanding – not a person, it's been said, who would suffer fools gladly, or indeed, if at all.

The Chairman was Colonel John Graham McKerlie, who, according to his obituary in the *Minutes and Proceedings of the Institute of Civil Engineers*, 'carried out the duties of his post with in wearying zeal, and in times of political and agrarian troubles, even at personal risk'. His courtesy and kindness, according to the *Dictionary of Irish Architects*, 'gained for him the title of "the poor man's friend".' He was a keen sportsman, a painter and an art lover, and for a time served as a Governor of the National Gallery of Ireland.

The third Commissioner is the most interesting: William le Fanu, younger brother of the novelist J. Sheridan le Fanu. An engineer, he was apprenticed to John Benjamin McNeill, the great railway engineer, and had been involved in the construction of the Great Southern and Western Railway. He was the designer of the Bagenalstown and Ballywilliam line.

If his very readable memoir, *Seventy Years of Irish Life*, is to be believed, his arduous engineering and public service career did not prevent Le Fanu from having an enjoyable private life .He enjoyed fishing in particular, killing in his lifetime, by his own calculation, 1,295 salmon, 2,636 sea-trout and 65,436 river and lake-trout.

Though a member of the gentry, his relations with the country people were relaxed and friendly. Some were his friends and they trusted him with dark secrets. Brought to see an illicit still, something which he had never seen before, he was told how his illegal distilling acquaintances evaded the notice of the police: '[W]e always dry the malt in the beginning of July, when all the police are taken off to Derry to put down the riots there; so we can do it safely then. God is good, sir; God is good.'

Le Fanu was convivial, good-humoured and, as noted earlier, liked nothing better than to sit up till the small hours, drinking, singing and telling stories. His memoirs are full of these, very much of the Samuel Lover, proto-Somerville-and-Ross-type, but there are some interesting glimpses of pre-Famine Ireland; ferocious faction fights during which people actually died, and the dire housing conditions of the peasantry.

William Le Fanu (1816-1894)

His mother was 'a bit of a rebel' who, when a child, stole from the drawing room of Major Sirr – Mrs. Sirr was a relation – the dagger with which Lord Edward Fitzgerald defended himself during his last ultimately fatal encounter with Sirr. (Le Fanu himself eventually got possession of it.) The Sheares brothers were also family friends and in his memoirs Le Fanu reproduces a letter written by John Sheares to his own uncle the night before his execution.

Such, then, were those on whose recommendation permission was given to build a clubhouse in the southeast corner of Kingstown Harbour between the Mail Boat pier and the East Piers. In the absence of any documentation, what seems likely was that somehow on the chain between Kingstown Harbour and the Viceregal Lodge someone, somewhere, in the informal way these things happen, 'had a word' with someone else who mattered, so that eventually His Excellency the Lord Lieutenant would have had no trouble giving the required assent.

Curiously, at the club's inaugural meeting in November 1869, no one thought to mention that some of those present had been on a deputation that had met the Board of Work's chairman, Col. McKerlie, the previous day to discuss acquiring the site. 'They had left with the pleasing impression that their mission had been most successful,' to quote the *Freeman's Journal* on the 26th. Col. McKerlie had 'only a few points he wished to investigate.' And, finally, according to the *Freeman*, 'the Lord Mayor has consented to be one of the patrons of the new club and with the support already received, its success is certain.'

Handing over control of public property in a strategic location to a private club was (and still is) no easy matter, and Col. McKerlie would certainly have had the advice of his fellow-commissioner, who was in charge of harbours, William le Fanu. If the promoters of the club were seeking to plead their cause, le Fanu was their man. He was approachable and friendly and, what's more, he was also on very good personal terms with the Viceroy who would make the ultimate decision on the matter. At one stage they were to go fishing together but the arrangement fell through. Later, at a party in the Viceregal Lodge, he had entertained the company with a recitation penned for him by his brother Joe, the author of spooky stories like *The House by the Churchyard*.

You can actually see evidence of the final stage of the approval process in the side notes scribbled on the left hand side of to the letter to the Lord Lieutenant from the Office of Public Works dated 28 December 1869. Firstly, 'Lord Lieutenant – can this (illeg) be given?'

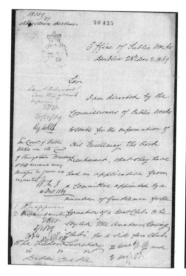  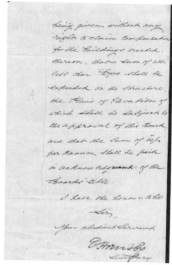

Board of Works Three Page Letter to the Viceroy, 28 December 1869

And, further down, 'The Commissioners of Public Works are the Commissioners of Kingstown Harbour and consent may therefore be given as requested'. And then, finally, '1. H.Ex .approves, 2. Prepare sanction. 8/1.'

The man who was Lord Lieutenant at the time – and to whom members of the National Yacht Club owe permission for the building of their clubhouse – was John Spencer, 5th Earl Spencer, great-grandfather of Diana, Princess of Wales. He had a difficult term of office in Ireland during the Gladstone regime, having to deal with the fallout from the Land Act of 1870 and the disestablishment of the Church of Ireland in 1869. He was instinctively liberal and was credited with the release of Fenian prisoners and the establishment of government tribunals to enforce fair rent on Irish landlords.

What is definitely not to his credit was his failure to pardon or release the unfortunate Myles Joyce, wrongly convicted of involvement in the Maamtrasna murders, when proof was emerging that Joyce was totally innocent. His chilling words, the night before the execution, 'the law must take its course', is another of those unfortunate utterances that continue to populate the charge-sheet of British misdeeds in Ireland.

The Office of Public Works' letter was addressed to the Under-Secretary in Dublin Castle, who at the time was Thomas Henry Burke (a friend of Le Fanu's, by the way, whom he refers to in his memoirs as 'Tom Burke'). The initials on the side notes are possibly Burke's. He has his own sad place in Irish history. He was assassinated by the Invincibles in May 1882, in the Phoenix Park, alongside Gladstone's nephew, Sir Frederick Cavendish. It was probably Burke who actually made the decision granting permission to build on the harbour site.

Described somewhere as 'the real ruler of the country', Burke was obviously an effective networker; it was through his intervention through personal contacts that serious conflicts didn't develop when evictions at Carraroe were about to take place. Unlike most other holders of the office, his own roots were deep in Irish history. He was a direct descendant of Sir Ulick Burke, the wily 1st Marquess of Clanrickarde, an active Stuart supporter and reportedly a skilled operator, who managed to survive the Cromwellian victory and recover his estates on the Stuart restoration. Diplomacy, obviously, was in the genes.

The letter itself is worth reproducing in full because it contains, in its final paragraph, a sting which no doubt caused some unease among members of an National Yacht Club committee more than ninety years later when the erection of a the car ferry building in the southeast corner of the harbour had become a real and dangerous possibility.

> Sir,
>
> I am directed by the Commissioners of Public Works to state for the information of His Excellency, the Lord Lieutenant, that they have had an application from a committee appointed by a number of gentlemen for the formation of a boat club to be styled the Amateur Rowing Club, for the site for a club and boathouse at Kingstown.
>
> I forward a copy of the chart of Kingstown Harbour showing the proposed site between the Mail packet Pier and the East

Piers, and I am directed to request if you will be good enough to obtain the sanction of His Excellency, the Lord Lieutenant, under the Act 1ˢᵗ Geo IV chap 69- section 10 to the commissioners granting a lease to the club on the following conditions viz:

That if the ground is at any time required for the Public Service it will be surrendered on three months' notice being given without any rights to claim compensation for the buildings erected thereon, that a sum not less than €700 shall be expended on the structure the plans of the elevation of which shall be subject to the approval of the Board and that the sum of 10/- per annum shall be paid in acknowledgement of the Board's title.

I have the honour to be sir, etc.

So, at the start of 1870, the promoters, Messrs. Brunker, Walshe, Creagh and Beatty, had received the authority to build a clubhouse at Kingstown Harbour. Its actual location was shown on the chart submitted with the application; it is clearly where the National Yacht Club stands today (see page 5). The fact that the body receiving the sanction, described in the application as an amateur rowing club, had, within a short space of time become a much more imposing Kingstown Royal Harbour Boat Club and which was building a large, elegant, commodious clubhouse, seems not to have caused raised eyebrows in any quarter.

4.

Beginnings

The plans are by Mr. William Stirling, architect, Great Brunswick
St. Mr. J. Cunningham, Dalkey, has commenced the first section
of the contract at £600. – Irish Builder 1 May 1870.

No one has ever thought to include William Stirling among the top flight of Irish architects of the nineteenth century. He was no John Skipton Mulvany, nor a Francis Johnston, nor a Richard Morrison. Nor was he a Thomas Deane (the elder) in whose office he worked in the 1860s before setting up his own practice.

Yet the National Yacht Club – one of the few buildings which can be definitely attributed to Stirling – is listed for preservation by the local authority and such is its odd charm and elegance that artists never tire of drawing or painting it. The club itself has five such paintings or drawings displayed in the members' bar. One of them is by the late Michael O'Herlihy, still remembered here as a competitive Dublin Bay sailor who first distinguished himself as a set designer for the Edwards-MacLiammoir company before sailing away to become a famous film director in Hollywood.

Stirling was something of an artist himself. Besides the architectural drawings which he regularly displayed at the annual RHA exhibitions, he also exhibited up to 250 landscape sketches for the Dublin Sketching group between 1876 and 1898. Readers of his curriculum vitae will get the impression that his was a restless talent that never fully lived up to its potential. During his Irish career, he moved between eight businss addresses and nine home addresses. In 1907, when he was in his late sixties, he left Ireland for India.

The *Irish Builder* adds that in January 1908, he was professionally engaged in Bombay but that he would 'shortly leave to take up a responsible position in Calcutta'. The *Dictionary of Irish Architects* surmises that the position in Calcutta may not have materialised, and in 1911 the *Irish Builder* reported that Stirling had moved to Colombo 'having previously been in Bombay ever since leaving Ireland several years ago'. He was 'ensconced in the Grand Hotel, Colombo, after which he disappears from view'.

Too much should not be read into Stirling's frequent changes of residence. For people in comfortable circumstances at that time, moving house frequently was the acepted norm – indeed, rental income provided pensions for many retired persons in nineteenth century Dublin. Re-locating frequently did not necessarily indicate a rackety temperament, or an inability to earn a steady income. Dublin Bay Sailing Club's first Hon. Secretary, P.J. O'Connor Glynn, a first division clerk in Guiness' Brewery, a steady job if ever there was one, changed house much more frequently than his present-day counterparts – or their wives – would consider normal.

It is also true, of course, that jobs in the building industry are traditionally more subject to the ebbs and flows of economic activity than other occupations. Stirling may in that repect not have been much different from any present-day architect. In lean times he seems to have got by by accepting positions as surveyor to the Pembroke Township, the Rathdown Union, and probably the Clontarf Township as well.

But thanks to the National Yacht Club there remains at least one substantial building to perpetuate the memory of this sadly disregarded figure. Peter Pearson, in his history of Dún Laoghaire, noted that Stirling's design for the exterior of the club suggests a hybrid French chateau, hunting lodge or garden pavilion. He refers to 'units of three pedimented bays containing rounded windows and blank roundels'. He adds: 'The continuity of these elements with the elegant chimney stacks of the building gave a certain grace and unity.'

Another approach would be to forget about hybrid French chateaux or hunting lodges and just regard the building in its own terms: a simple, attractive structure very much in keeping with the tastes and requirement of its middle-class promoters; no classical flourishes, no balustrades, no arcades, no pillars. Yet the tall, round-headed windows in the front elevation, alternating in each of the three pedimented bays with rectangular windows, have a certain Palladian air which goes to soften what otherwise might be an overly austere exterior. You can easily understand why the relevant authorites would be keen to have it classified as a protected strcture.

From the bandstand on the East Pier, the public view of the rear elevation since Stirling's day has changed totally. A balcony has been added, not to mention an extensive forecourt which effectively hides from sight the lower stories. Set comfortably in the southeast corner of Dún Laoghaire harbour, the building manages to hold its own against the towering presence of the Lexicon in the background.

The promoters, to give them their due, showed commendable courage in setting about such an undertaking. Substantial citizens as they might have been, none of their occupations, at first glance, would suggest that they were in a category that had easy access to what some might descibe nowadays as serious money.

And the new club was certainly going to require a lot of it. The building was originally supposed to cost £2,000, which then, in the way these things happen, somehow grew to £4,000. A back-of-an-

East Pier before building

envelope calculation would suggest that today such a structure would cost – if you were lucky – around £4 million. You have to admire the promoters' pluck, vision and self-confidence.

And they seem to have had it in abundance. A few months before the stone-laying ceremony – on 9 February – having learnt that a rumour was circulating that a split had taken place resulting in a great secession from the club, they issued a spirited denial printed in *The Irish Times*:

> Permit me to assure our friends that such is not the case; that we are increasing beyond expectaton,and have not lost a single member since the club was formed, but one who resigned from private motives. All the reports are *canards*, issued by a set of disappointed applicants for admission, our success causing their jealousy.

Much the behind-the-scenes work had already taken place before the opening ceremony. A building committee had been quickly set up and, according to the *Irish Builder* in its issue of 15 February, they were inviting tenders for the 'erection of the foundation, basement and boat-stores of a club house and the formation of a boat-slip at Kingstown, from the plans of Mr. W. Stirling, architect.'

Accessing finance would have been the major concern of the committee which, on 26 May, just over a month after the laying of the first stone, had speedily got down to business. John Beatty, one of the two Hon. Secretaries (the other was the afore-mentioned Francis Lucas Cadwallader Walshe), was the assistant manager of the Royal Bank in Kingstown and would probably have been of some of some help with securing short-term funding to deal with immediate requirements. William Brooke Beatty, a family member, who was a bullion dealer besides an agent for a number of insurance companies, would also have been of assistance. Masonic contacts may have helped as well as nearly all who were prominently involved in the project were masons – Thomas Brunker belonged to the Duke of Clarence Lodge (No.171), both James and William Beatty belonged to Lodge No. 6 and Simon Creagh belonged to Lodge No. 666 (Dublin**).

The *Irish Builder*, in its issue dated 1 May, just over a week after the first-stone laying ceremony, reported that the contractor, Mr. J. Cunningham from Dalkey, had already commenced the first part of the contract at £600. (Cunningham, by the way, lived in Dalkey on – where else ? – Cunningham Road.)

Cunningham was indeed an 'eminent and well-known builder' as stated by *The Irish Times*. He built the Stillorgan reservoir, a number of railway bridges and viaducts as well as the quay at Coliemore Harbour. So it can be presumed that the money to pay Mr. Cunningham for this part of the project was already in place ('a respectable sum' had been raised before the stone-laying cereminy – £380, in fact).What the Committee had to concern itself with at this point was funding in the longer term.

Their solution, as in the case of the Royal Irish Yacht Club and other clubs as well, was a loan debenture, structured so as to protect the officers of the club. One of the original certificates has survived. It's displayed in the clubhouse on the landing of the stairway to the lower storey. It's worth a glance (see image on page 28). This is how it reads:

LOAN DEBENTURE

Whereas the Society or Club called 'The Kingstown Royal Harbour Boat Club' are possessed of a certain Plot of Ground, situate at the Harbour of Kingstown, in the County of Dublin, under a lease thereof made by the Commissioners of Public Works in Ireland to Thomas Brunker, of Idrone Terrace, Blackrock; F.L.C. Walshe, of Crofton Road, Kingstown; and Simon Creagh and James Beatty, both of Royal Terrace, West, Kingstown, gentlemen, and dated the the twenty-first day of January, one thousand, eight hundred and seventy one.

And whereas a Club-house and offices are now being erected upon said Plot of ground, by and for the use of the members of said Club; and by a resolution of said Club, bearing date the 26th day of May 1870, - It was ordered that the Committee be empowered to raise a sum of Two Thousand Pounds by debentures to bear interest at the rate of six per cent per annum and when such sum when so raised, or so much thereof as should be necessary for the purpose, should be applied towards the creation and completion of the said Club-house and Offices.

Now in pursuance of the said resolution, and on behalf of the said committee, and in consideration of one hundred pounds stg. paid by Jerome O'Flaherty, of 101 Upper Georges St., Kingstown, to the Treasurer of said club, testified by hi signing the receipt for same at the foot hereof, we, the Honorary Secretaries, and Treasurer do hereby declare that the said sum of one hundred pounds is hereby made, and is henceforth a charge upon the funds and the assets of said Club, said sum to bear interest at the rate of Six per cent per annum until the repayment of said principal sum of one hundred pounds stg. to Jerome O'Flaherty, his executors, administrators or assigns, such interest to be paid half-yearly on every first day of January and the first day of July each year.

Provided that it shall not be lawful for any Debenture holder to sell, assign, or give away any such debenture to any person

Kingstown Royal Harbour Boat Club.

LOAN DEBENTURE.

Whereas the Society or Club called "The Kingstown Royal Harbour Boat Club" are possessed of a certain Plot of Ground, situate at the Harbour of Kingstown, in the County of Dublin, under a lease thereof made by the Commissioners of Public Works in Ireland to THOMAS BRUNKER, of Idrone Terrace, Blackrock; FRANCIS L. C. WALSHE, of Crofton Road, Kingstown; and SIMON CREAGH and JAMES BEATTY, both of Royal Terrace, West, Kingstown, gentlemen, and dated the twenty-first day of January, one thousand eight hundred and seventy-one.

And whereas a Club-house and Offices are now being erected upon said Plot of ground, by and for the use of the Members of said Club; and by a Resolution of said Club, bearing date the 26th day of May, 1870,—It was ordered that their Committee be empowered to raise a sum of Two Thousand Pounds by Debentures to bear interest at the rate of six per cent. per annum, and that said sum when so raised, or so much thereof as should be necessary for the purpose, should be applied towards the erection and completion of the said Club-house and Offices.

Now, in pursuance of the said resolution, and on behalf of said Committee, and in consideration of the sum of *One Hundred Pounds Stg* paid by *Jerome C Flaherty M.D.* of *101 Upper Georges St. Kingstown* to the Treasurer of said Club, testified by his signing the receipt for same at foot hereof, We, the Honorary Secretaries and Treasurer, do hereby declare that the said sum of *One Hundred Pounds Sterling* is hereby made, and is henceforth a charge upon the funds and other assets of said Club, said sum to bear interest at the rate of Six Pounds per cent. per annum until the repayment of said principal sum of *One Hundred Pounds Stg* to the said *Jerome C Flaherty* his executors, administrators, or assigns, such interest to be paid half-yearly on every first day of January and first day of July in each year.

PROVIDED ALWAYS that it shall not be lawful for any Debenture holder to sell, assign, or give over any such Debenture to any person other than a Member of said Club; and also provided that no personal liability shall attach to the said Honorary Secretaries or Treasurer, they executing this Debenture solely as Officers of the Club in trust for said Club. And it is hereby agreed upon, that the holder of this Debenture shall await payment until such payment comes to his turn by lottery, such lottery to be regulated by the General Committee of the Club, save as hereinafter mentioned—that is to say, that in the event of the death of any Debenture holder, that his personal representative shall be at liberty to demand payment from the Committee of the Club; and if not paid within three months of such demand, shall be at liberty to sell and dispose of same to such person as such representative shall think proper.

AND IT IS FURTHER AGREED UPON, that all Debentures issued and to be issued in pursuance of the foregoing resolution, shall not have priority one over another, but that all shall have equal priority.

Given under our hands and the Seal of the Club, this ____ day of _____ , 1871.

Received from the above-named *Jerome C Flaherty M.D.*
the sum of *One Hundred Pounds Sterling*
being the consideration for said Debenture.

£ 1 0 0 0   } Treasurer.
Countersigned.

} Honorary Secretaries.

Loan Debenture, 1871

other than a member said Club; and also provided that no personal liability shall attach to the said Honorary Secretaries or treasurer, they executing this debenture solely as officers of the club in trust for said Club.

And it is hereby agreed upon, that the holder of this debenture shall await payment until such payment comes to him by lottery, to be regulated by the General Committee of the club, save as hereinafter mentioned – that is to say that in the event of the death of any Debenture holder, that his personal representative shall be at liberty to demand payment for the Committee of the Club, and if not paid within three months of such demand shall be at liberty to sell and dispose to such personas such representative shall think proper.

And it is hereby agreed upon that all debentures issued and to be issued in pursuance of the foregoing resolution shall not have priority one over another, but that all shall have equal priority. Given under our seal of the Club etc.

So, with funding arrangements in place, and fortified by the goodwill of their noble patron and well-placed friends in local business and professional circles, the promoters looked forward to a happy future for the club.

A cheering portent of things to come was the following notice on the 15 June 1871 in the *Freeman's Journal*:

The new building constructed for this club by Mr. John Cunningham, the contractor of Dalkey, from designs by Mr. Stirling, C.E. is expected to open for the reception of members by the 1st. June.

But goodwill and enthusiasm will only go so far. The first three decades of the club, and its transformations under various names, were to prove much more daunting than Messrs. Brunker, Beatty, Walshe and Creagh could ever have visualised.

5.

Trials and Tribulations, 1870-1887

Queens Road, Kingstown, c. 1880

Given the fervent backing of 'people of wealth and rank', as Mr. Crosthwaite termed them, it would seem curious that, during the first two decades of its existence, things did not turn out at all well for the new club.

Support for rowing was to be the club's *raison d'être*, a sport that at the time excited great public interest. You can get a flavour of this in the *Freeman's Journal's* report on the Metropolitan regatta at Ringsend in April 1874. There were huge crowds, many of them arriving on foot, as well as the usual assembly of fashionable ladies 'fair and beautiful', not to speak of music provided by the band of the 17th Lancers.

The *Freeman's* correspondent was a bit grumpy about the venue – a shipping neighbourhood, dingy and grimy with colliers lying unsightly at anchor and smoke belching from tall chimneys, compensated, it was true, by the seaward view of Dublin Bay, with Howth on it northern shore and Killiney on its southern.

To give them their due, the home team developed a routine to attract the public to their own activities by running races alongside the East Pier inside Kingstown Harbour. All this, in addition to attending 'away' events, at which Mr. W.B. Brooks, one of the club's founding fathers, was a keen, and sometimes successful, participant. Another name which appears in reports of these events was a Mr. R.G. O'Flaherty, of whom more presently.

The personnel of the club's officer board did not change much in those early years. In 1874, Mr. William C. Hogan became Honorary Secretary and Mr. Robertson Jones Honorary Treasurer. In that year, too, the Earl of Longford became President. It can be presumed that the club at this stage was being run like any other gentleman's club. A George Lynch had been appointed House Steward (presumably living-in, like the house stewards in the other clubs) and there had also been press advertisements looking for an under-waiter and a billiard-marker.

But unaccountably, despite all the initial enthusiasm, the club failed to prosper. Perhaps rowing was not a sport that required a clubhouse on such a scale. Or perhaps the founders lacked the necessary experience. Or perhaps more likely, being busy professional men, they simply hadn't the time to devote sufficient attention to what at the outset was a fairly formidable business challenge.

Later, it emerged that at a time when club membership was at its peak, numbering about 200, it had been necessary to impose a compulsory 'whip' whereby members were obliged to pay £5 by the end of the year, failing which their membership ceased. This was bit steep, given that the initial membership subscription was two guineas. The following year there had been another 'whip' – voluntary this time – which realised some money, but members were becoming increasingly disenchanted. By early 1880 with membership fallen to just 60, it had become clear that the club was insolvent and unable to pay its creditors.

The sad state of the club's finances came into sharp relief on the 3 December 1880 when the Master of the Rolls had before him the case – presumably non-payment of debts – of *Jones v Beatty*. Mr D. O'Riordan, QC, along with Mr Arthur Houston, QC, instructed by Mr Simon Creagh, had moved for an order that the club be wound up. (Mr Creagh, so it happened, was one of the founding members.)

The affairs of the club were discussed at some length during the hearing, resulting in the court's conclusion that, as admitted by Mr Creagh, the true cause of the failure was the sharp rise in the costs of belonging to the club. Why the Committee found it necessary to increase fees was not gone into.

Accordingly, there was no choice but for the Master of the Rolls to declare, 'Let the club be wound up, as prayed'. He did so, he said, with some sadness, having often admired the clubhouse during his walks on the pier. He trusted some effort would be made to revive it and make provision for 'this most legitimate and noble sport'.

Among the names of the club officers quoted in a liquidation notice published in the press on the 1 February 1881 was that of Thomas Brunker (who, it might be recalled, made the silver trowel presented to Lord Longford at the first stone-laying ceremony in 1870). Mr. Brunker was not having a happy time of it in those years: on 24 September 1879, his shop at 111 Grafton Street, fell into the street, which effectively put him out of business. He sued his next door neighbour, North's, the house agents and estate valuers, who, allegedly caused the collapse while having work done on their own premises. He looked for £7,200 but was awarded £900 – an amount which pleased neither party, according to the *Irish Builder* in December 1880.

Of some note is the court's observation that a factor which limited the value of the clubhouse was the clause in the original lease that the structure built on it was to have similar objectives to the original club. Needless to add, many generations of club members have owed much to the foresight of the members of the Board of Works who inserted this most useful and important clause.

After the liquidation things took their inevitable course. On 29 April 1881, Messrs. Talbot Coall & Son, auctioneers, 13 Upper Georges Street, Kingstown, announced that the auction of the clubhouse and its effects would take place on 21 May. This duly happened and control of the clubhouse and effects passed to a new set of owners – a syndicate whose intention was to make a profit from it. The purchase price was £1,250.

Their motives were of the highest, if you can believe a report in the *Freeman's* of 27 June:

> The purchasers are gentlemen thoroughly interested in the progress of Kingstown and are determined to make the club one of the chief attractions of the township. The club will be opened on a most liberal basis providing an intellectual resort for gentlemen of the locality and also amusement for the district.

(Meaning, perhaps, that there would be no black-balling, provided you were a gentleman with a taste for elevated discourse.)

The syndicate set to work in a thoroughly business-like fashion. Soon after the purchase – July 1881 – they started to manage the premises as a 'proprietary' club under the name of the Kingstown Yacht Club. Income would be derived from members' subscriptions and profits on the sale of liquor. This was a pivotal moment. From that point on, the club, rather than being a body devoted solely to the sport of rowing, became a yacht club. Promotion of rowing was included as one of the two objectives of the club, a necessary provision since some shares had been allotted to the former proprietors and rowing, of course, still continued to be a popular pastime.

It took some time to draft the memorandum of agreement setting up the company but it was finally signed on 10 December 1882 by the syndicate's six members and new partner, Thomas Baker. Registration of the company followed on 3 February 1883, with limited liability. From then on the club became The Kingstown Yacht Club Ltd., although for sailing purposes the word 'limited' was dropped.

The new team set about organising racing with commendable zest and efficiency. A Notice of Race for a series of nine races to be held in the summer of 1882 miraculously survived the club fire of 1975 – you can read it on the landing of the stairs to the club's ground floor. It is signed by a Hamilton Leslie, who was probably a kinsman of Captain Peacocke, the syndicate's leading light. His occupation was given in one of the directories as 'emigration agent', which used to be someone who selected tenants of distressed estates for assistance to emigrate.

The sailing programme outlined in the Notice of Race was certainly an ambitious undertaking for a new club. The yachting press gave encouraging coverage with the *Freeman's Journal's* yachting correspondent referring on 17 July to 'this now flourishing club'. Although he did find things to criticize. 'The hour for starting,' he wrote, 'was 2:30 sharp, according to the town clock, but the binocular of the starter must have been adrift and it was exactly 3:45 when the yachts were dispatched.'

The *Freeman's* correspondent went on a bit about the lack of support: 'Whatever cynics may say, we augur a future for the Kingstown Yacht Club which at present may seem ephemeral. Their programme is good, their system is good, and in a few years the Kingstown Club, as a small yachting club, will rank about the best in the kingdom – that is, if it be only properly supported.'

The lack of support was indeed notable: turnout rarely exceeded three boats, and for the first race there were no entries at all.

Of some interest is a name mentioned in the 1882 Notice of Race. Competing boats which were looking for crew were asked to contact a Dr. O'Flaherty 'at the club'. The name keeps cropping up throughout most of the club's early history from that inaugural meeting in 1869, then the first debenture certificate issued in 1871 to a Jerome O'Flaherty, then the Kingstown Yacht Club period, and finally to post-1901, when the club had become the Edward Yacht Club. It shows there existed a continuity of sorts throughout the various vicissitudes that the club was destined to undergo.

The leading personality of the syndicate was Captain Peter Leslie Peacocke who had addresses at 36 Bride Street and Villagio, Dalkey. Like nearly everyone else involved in the club's early

KINGSTOWN YACHT CLUB 1882

PROGRAMME.

First Match — Saturday, 10th June. Yachts not exceeding 3 Tons. First Prize, £3. Second Prize, £1.

Second Match — Saturday, 17th June. Open Boats. Prize, £2.

Third Match — Saturday, 1st July. (Corinthian) Sealed Handicap for Yachts not exceeding 3 Tons. Prize, £4 for Helmsman and Crew.

Fourth Match — Saturday, 8th July. Open Boats. Prize, £2.

Fifth Match — Saturday, 15th July. Sealed Handicap for Yachts not exceeding 3 Tons. First Prize, £3. Second Prize, £1.

Sixth Match — Tuesday, 18th July. Yachts not exceeding 10 Tons. First Prize, £7. Second Prize, £3.

Seventh Match — Wednesday, 19th July. Yachts not exceeding 5 Tons. First Prize, £4. Second Prize, £1.

Eighth Match — Thursday, 20th July. Yachts not exceeding 3 Tons. First Prize, £3. Second Prize, £1.

Ninth Match — Friday, 21st July. Yachts not exceeding 3 Tons. First Prize, £3. Second Prize, £1.

Tenth Match — Saturday, 22nd July. Yachts not exceeding 5 Tons. First Prize, £4. Second Prize, £1.

Eleventh Match — Saturday, 29th July. (Corinthian) Yachts not exceeding 3 Tons. Prize, £4 for Helmsman and Crew.

Twelfth Match — Saturday, 5th August. Sealed Handicap for Yachts not exceeding 3 Tons. First Prize, £3. Second Prize, £1.

Thirteenth Match — Saturday, 12th August. Open Boats. Prize, £2.

Total, First Prizes ... £42
Do. Second Prizes ... 12

Total ... £54

10-Ton Course—24 Miles.   5-Ton Course—12 Miles.   3-Ton Course—9 Miles.   Course for Open Boats to be named on day of Match.

SAILING REGULATIONS.

TIME WILL BE TAKEN FROM THE TOWN HALL CLOCK.

All Matches shall be sailed under the Rules of the Yacht Racing Association (except as hereinafter provided). All Prizes shall be for Yachts of 10 Tons and under, and for Open Boats belonging to Members only, in classes according to their tonnage and length of keel respectively.

In all Matches, Yachts and Boats shall be worked by its Members, or their sons under 18 years of age, or by Members of Yacht Clubs whose station is at least 50 miles from Kingstown, save one paid hand, which shall be allowed to each Yacht or Boat, none but a Member to steer. For the conducting of all Matches the Committee shall appoint an Officer of the Day, who shall have the entire management in respect to starting, taking time, &c., and shall have power to postpone the Race, should the weather, in his opinion, be unfit, or likely to become unfit for sailing the Race, either to a later hour of the same day or to another day, as he may think expedient. In the event of a dispute as to tonnage, Yachts to be measured at the expense of the party in error.

In all Matches Yachts to be started underway.

The Owner, if on board during a Match, shall be held responsible that all rules of the Club shall be strictly observed, or, in his absence, the Member who acts as his representative.

In case of a protest being lodged with the Officer of the Day, the person making same shall deposit with him the sum of Ten Shillings, to be returned in case protest is held good; otherwise to become forfeit to the funds of the Club. All protests to be made in writing within two hours of termination of the Match.

Any Yacht entered for a Race, and not starting, shall be fined Ten Shillings.

All Entries must be made in writing to the Secretary, at least two days previous to the day of the Match.

Owners wanting amateur crews for the Matches, and gentlemen wishing for berths, are requested to communicate with Dr. R. G. O'Flaherty, at the Club.

No Second Prize will be given in any Match unless three Boats start.

Notice of Race, Kingstown Yacht Club, 1882

history, he was a Mason – originally the Shakespeare Lodge (No. 143) and, from 1880, the Dalkey Lodge (No 261). His mother Sarah was one of the Leslies, a well-heeled south County Dublin family whose original family home was at Woodley, Stillorgan. The house is still there, on the Upper Kilmacud Road, but much altered since the Leslies owned it.

The Leslie connection is of some interest (and to the Peacockes, of considerable consequence). Though they had property in Fermanagh, most of the Leslie money came from pharmaceuticals. They were wholesale chemists, with a very profitable business at 36 Bride Street, supplying, among others, many local dispensaries and workhouses. Sarah's brother, Charles Leslie, ran the business after his father had died. He never married and on his death in October 1879 his interests passed to his nephews, namely, our Peter Leslie Peacocke and his elder brother, Thomas Goodriche Peacocke (who, just to make things complicated, was named exactly as his father).

This elder brother inherited Carraig na Greine in Dalkey, a property of some style. It now houses the Sue Ryder Foundation on Coliemore Road.

Uncle Charles, according to E. McDowel Cosgrave in *Dublin and County Dublin* in *the 20th Century*, used to put the demesne at the disposal of the Viceroy and his family 'as a mark of respect to the representative of her late Majesty, Queen Victoria'. Peter, on the other hand, inherited the Leslie pharmaceutical business at 36 Bride Street.

Other members of the syndicate, as listed in an 1887 memorial of assignment, were Richard J. Donnelly, C.J. Fay, a solicitor, John Stuart Stevenson, Patrick A. O'Farrell, and James Henry Fay. A group of worthy men, by all accounts, but they don't appear to have worked happily together. For example, one of them, a wine merchant, took an action against his fellow members over the profit he was making on supplying wine to the club. But the main culprit, you have to suspect, must have been Captain Peter Leslie Peacocke who, whatever his other merits, turned out to be have been the most awkward, if not the most litigious, of men.

Carraig na Greine, now owned by the Sue Ryder Foundation

In 1884, C.J. Fay and Peacocke fell out over the running costs of the latter's yacht *Ellah*, having acquired the vessel on the understanding that the two of them would share the costs. The dispute ended up in the Exchequer Court on 26 November. Fay's object in taking a share of the yacht, it emerged, had been in the interest of his wife's health, but when she found that persons to whose presence she objected had been taken on board she could not, and did not, make use of the yacht. Fay counter-claimed, looking for £250 from Peacocke for mismanagement of the yacht. (Peacocke won the case on points of law.)

Who these objectionable persons might have been was not mentioned in court, either because it was irrelevant or because everybody already knew. Obviously it was someone who mattered a lot to Peacocke since he was prepared to go to court about it.

A possible candidate might be his second son, Lieutenant Leslie Tufnell Peacocke, who at this stage might have been exhibiting the character deficiencies that were later exposed in a very lurid way in the House of Lords. (A special bill had to be brought before the Lords to dissolve his marriage to the beautiful Beatrice Isabel Lloyd, of Victoria Castle, later Ayesha Castle. Lieutenant Peacocke had been singularly ungracious towards his wife, pushing her down the stairs, locking her out of the bedroom, pouring water over her, trampling over her clothes and throwing her ring in the fire. He was also a serial adulterer.) Or perhaps it was *both* Peacockes whose presence disturbed Mrs. Fay.

On another occasion Peacocke took a libel action against the *Medical Press*, which had said unkind things about the quality of the medicines his firm was supplying to two of the Poor Law Unions. In fairness to Peacocke, it must be added that at a meeting of one of the unions there was the suggestion that the complaint originated with a competitor. Then, there was the court case about the tardy renewal of a seasonal railway ticket between him and the Dublin, Wicklow and Wexford Railway Co. – the court found that Peacocke had been technically at fault but was prompted to observe that he had not acted in an ungentlemanly fashion.

He didn't get on well either with some of his Dalkey neighbours. He was living in Villagio, a villa adjoining his brother's demesne, Carraig na Greine, and had blocked off public access to a well at the foot of the demesne. With the coming of the Dartry water-scheme the well had lost its importance and the tunnel and connecting laneway were accumulating some noxious refuse. Peacocke claimed he had got the verbal permission of the Dalkey Commissioners to block access but no one remembered it and, anyway, there was no legal, written permission. The whole affair, which was revealed in the *Freeman's Journal*, generated a lot of bad feeling locally.

With the syndicate's members so much at odds and there being no great interest in their sailing programme, failure was inevitable. The truth was, as was frankly admitted during the liquidation hearing, that there was no one really interested in carrying on the business of the club. On 19 January 1887, Richard Donnelly, the original member and wine merchant mentioned above, applied to the Master of the Rolls to have it wound up. Some additional information on the club's finances was mentioned in court. Ms Phillipson & Smith, who were creditors of the club for £181, had been declared bankrupt the previous October, and nearly all the shareholders owed the company

Captain Peacocke's Dalkey residence, Villagio, still, exists, though much altered. Currently there are two dwellings on the site. The sea-facing house, overlooking Dalkey Sound, now owned by an NYC member, Marcus Higgins and family, is probably where Peacocke resided.

money. Mr C.J. Fay, Peacocke's former boat partner who had been an MP, had also become bankrupt.

The appeal was opposed on legal grounds by other members of the syndicate, namely Stevenson and Peacocke, and was adjourned to allow meetings between the parties to take place. Several adjournments ensued to enable the shareholders to decide on a voluntary wind-up or for a winding up under the supervision of the court. No compromise being in prospect, the Master of the Rolls got impatient and gave an order on 8 March 1887 for the company to be wound up. Later, on 2 July 1887, the Official Liquidator announced that he was prepared to accept tenders for the purchase of the Kingstown Yacht Club (in liquidation).

In fairness to the memory of Peacocke and Co. it should be added that economic circumstances at the time were not propitious, to put it mildly. Mary E. Daly, Professor of Modern history at UCD, and author of *Dublin: The Deposed Capital* notes that 'there was actually a global recession, bad especially for agriculture and land values – so had a severe impact in Ireland'.

The misfortunes of the club do not seem to have impacted on the affairs of the Leslie-Peacocke undertaking in Bride Street, nor indeed should they. Peter carried on with it until 1904 when he disposed it to a rival pharmaceutical company called Hunt. For a number of years he continued living at Villagio in Dalkey but for people of his background Ireland was becoming a place uncongenial to his whole outlook and mode of life.

His military service was with a smart cavalry regiment, the Queen's 16th Lancers, with deployment on the Empire's borders, on the Indian North-Western frontier. His first son, Leslie Tufnell Peacocke, was born in 1868 in India. When he actually left Ireland is unclear but it was in Christchurch, Somerset that he died in 1917 and where he was presumably interred – far from the final resting places of most of his immediate Peacocke and Leslie family – in the churchyard of St. Brigid's, Stillorgan.

6.

Charles Barrington and the Absolute Club

Charles Barrington (1834-1901)

Last night the gentlemen cricketers of Philadelphia, who are engaged to play the University Past and Present today and tomorrow, and the Gentlemen of Ireland on the next two days, were entertained at a banquet by the members of the Absolute Club.

It was one of the most successful and sociable dinners ever held in Ireland and when it is noted that Mr Charles B. Barrington was in the chair, people may readily realise what the administration was like…. The catering was excellent, reflecting great credit on the steward, and the band of the 11th Hussars played most pleasantly during the dinner.

Afterwards, the string band of the Gasparres attended in the cardroom and were competent successors to the military......

Speechmaking was then concluded, when a move was made to the cardroom, where some real 'live' songs were rendered with ringing choruses. In this department Mr.L'Estrange was quite brilliant with his singing, whistling and imitations of brass instruments, and Mr J. M.Melden 'raised the rafters' with 'Ballyhooley'. Mr. McCarthy gave 'Killaloe' and several others were hard at it, the fun being fairly 'moving' when our representative was obliged to leave (*Freeman's Journal*, 2 July 1889).

There now enters upon the scene – and this can be said without much fear of contradiction – the most colourful person ever to have become involved in the story of the National Yacht Club. His name was Charles Barrington, of a Quaker family, of Fassaroe, Bray. They were high achievers, the Barringtons. Charles' half-sister, Amy, became an eminent scientist, working beside figures such as Francis Galton in the then-fashionable field of eugenics, and his brother Richard wrote scientific papers that were published in the journals of the Royal Irish Academy.

Charles' achievements were of a more physical, not to say, literal variety. He was the first ever to climb the Eiger (on 11 August 1858), clambering up the west flank against the vehement objections of his guides, not to mention the horror of the guides' families, who thought they were all going to be killed. He was so casual about claiming credit for this achievement that subsequent researchers had to rely on his signature in the guides' log books before satisfying themselves that he was indeed the climber who had attained the summit of the mountain.

Climbing the Eiger was an after-thought, apparently – a couple of days earlier he had climbed the Jungfrau (4,158 metres). He would have proceeded to climb the Matterhorn, were it not for the inconvenient fact that he had run out of money.

His next remarkable achievement was to win the first Irish Grand National on 4 April 1870 with his horse *Sir Robert Peel*, of which he was both trainer and jockey. He raced under an assumed name on that occasion to conceal his identity, probably from his family circle who would not all have approved of horse-racing and its connection with gambling. In that year, too, he organised the first Irish mountain race up the Sugar Loaf, for which he awarded a gold watch as a prize.

Taking over the then unsuccessful Kingstown Yacht Club to run it as a commercial undertaking was consistent with Barrington's sunny, can-do outlook. The Memorial of Assignment, following the liquidation of the Kingstown Yacht Club in July of 1887, is dated 21 December of that year. It's quite an elaborate document, naming up to twenty persons, divided into parties of the First, Second, Third, Fourth and Fifth parts. The location of the property is very clearly defined:

> All that piece or parcel of ground it situate lying and being between the Mail Steam Packet and East Pier of Kingstown Harbour containing in front to the road one hundred and eleven feet and alike number of feet in front to the said harbour and in flank from the front at low water fifty five feet.

Nowhere in the document is money mentioned and indeed, over the seventeen years that Barrington had custody of the building is not at all clear where the funding to acquire it came from. The actual money he paid for the clubhouse and accessories was noted in the press on 12 July 1887:

> The Master of the Rolls yesterday heard an application by the liquidator of the Kingstown Yacht Club to sanction a proposal by Mr. Charles Barrington for the purchase of the club properties for £1300. The Master of the Rolls sanctioned the application.

He was the moving spirit of two clubs in Dublin, the Ormond and the Sheridan. Both were situated at 23 St. Stephen's Street, not far from the United Services Club (No. 9) and next door to the

Friendly Brothers of St. Patrick (No. 22). *Thoms Directory* shows Charles as being both Treasurer and Secretary of the Sheridan Club.

Barrington's family business was soap making. It was a very successful undertaking, set up at 202 Great Britain Street (now Parnell Street) by a forebear, John Barrington. Over the years it became one of the most important industries in Dublin, becoming a limited liability company in 1890 under the title of John Barrington and Sons Ltd. It has a mention in *Ulysses*, with Leopold Bloom washing his hands 'in a tablet of Barrington's lemon-flavoured soap'.

Besides all his other activities, Barrington seems to have worked there. *Thoms* in 1897 shows him as living – or perhaps having an office beside – the main family business of soap manufacturing at 201/202 Great Britain Street. When he acquired his first boat that same address was quoted in *Lloyd's Yacht Register* though later entries listed his home address as 18 Earlsfort Terrace. Both addresses are recorded in the probate transcript of his will in 1901.

There is no record of the club having run into financial trouble when Barrington had control of it. On the contrary, he brought with him an entrepreneurial flair so markedly lacking among the previous owners. This innovative ability was noted by a columnist in the weekly *Irish Society* on 19 October 1889: 'The Absolute Club has proved a great success owing to its admirable management and has now a large number of members.'

This was partly achieved by Barrington quite openly canvassing for members among existing clubs. His programme was set out in a press advertisement on 14 March 1889:

The Absolute Club, Kingstown

It is intended to open this club of the season on the 1st April. Membership of this club is by invitation of the committee and anyone desirous of joining can become a member on receiving an invitation from the committee and paying his subscription, £2 2s. Any member, however of the following clubs-

The Friendly Brothers
The Kildare-street Club

The Royal Irish Yacht Club
The Royal St. George Yacht Club
The Sackville-street Club
The Sheridan Club
The Stephen's -green Club
The United Services Club, or
The University Club
may at once become a member on payment of the subscription, £2 2s. And members non-resident in Ireland of recognized English clubs can at once become members on payment of the subscription, £1 1s. Officers on full pay in the Army and Navy and Royal Irish Constabulary are eligible for membership at the subscription of £1 1s.

The club will be open during the yachting season. No member is entitled to membership for more than the current year as the committee will issue fresh invitations before the commencement of each season.

The club-house is conveniently situated near the East Pier, Kingstown, on the water's edge, and is admirably adapted to the needs of yachting and boating men. A number of boats will be kept for the use of members at a fixed charge. There is a first-class billiard-room, dining-room, and reading-room, where the daily and weekly papers will be found. The boathouse, which is large and well-lighted, faces the harbour and has been fitted-up for dancing, afternoon tea, music &c.

All communications should be made before the 1st of April, and all subscriptions should be made payable to the Hon. Secretary, who will be glad to afford any further information if required.

Women's membership, of course was not provided for but otherwise Barrington showed none of the sexism that was so markedly a feature of club life at the time (and afterwards, indeed, of the Edward Yacht Club). He was free from prejudice of any sort and made it clear from the outset that women would be welcome at the club.

The correspondent of *Irish Society* wrote on 20 April 1889:

The Absolute Club, Kingstown, has opened its doors for the season of 1889. Many improvements have been carried out during the months it has been closed and is now as comfortable a club as can be found in England, Scotland, or Ireland. Ladies highly appreciate the afternoon teas that can be dispensed there. They are perfect.

The club's afternoon teas received an equally enthusiastic notice on 22 March the following year:

The hospitable doors of the Absolute Club, Kingstown, will open on the 12th April. This will be agreeable news to many ladies, who, after *doing* the East pier on Sundays, love to turn into C.B.'s very pleasant club and have tea and fixings.

Concerts, balls and musical recitals were frequent events at the club during the Barrington regime as noted by *Irish Society's* correspondent in July 1889:

The Absolute Club will give a dance this (Wednesday) evening in their charmingly situated house. A special train in the early hours of tomorrow (Thursday) is announced to bring back to the Capital of Erin her fairest daughters and her bravest sons, though probably after indulging in the light fantastic for some hours they will not look their best.

Barrington, on one notable occasion showed highly uncommon civility towards sailors working on boats in the harbour. In July 1893 he invited 200 of them – plus girlfriends – to a splendid dance in the 'beautifully–floored' boat-house. Jane, the Kingstown correspondent of *Irish Society* (clearly a Barrington fan) wrote enthusiastically:

The sounding of the bell at midnight sent the men home to their ships – happy, sober and invigorated and, needless to say, full of gratitude to Mr. Barrington for his kindly interest in them, and generous desire for their enjoyment.

'C.B', as he is popularly called, thinks – as Jane does – that servants and employees of all kinds work well for those who are considerate and kind to them…there are unfortunately very few who, even in their own households, carry out so good a principle- and fewer far who, like 'CB', extend to those unconnected to them the courtesy and generosity which is all too seldom offered by employers.

(C.B.'s generosity, it will be noted, did not extend to free alcohol, possibly due to his Quaker principles, or else a shrewd awareness that sailors rowing back to their boats with drink taken was not a good idea.)

Barrington, on taking possession of the club at the end of 1887, also acquired his first boat, his brother John's 48 foot, 16 ton cutter, *Foam*. John was another of the Barrington high achievers. He was *Sir John Barrington*, Lord Mayor of Dublin in 1865 and again in 1879. The National Library's manuscript collection includes his account of cruises to the Low Countries and Scandinavia in 1868 and to the Clyde in 1872. The collection also includes some versification.

John's knighthood came from his contribution to the very successful Lord Mayor's Ball, held in the Mansion House during the visit of the Prince of Wales to the grand exhibition of 1865; it was attended, so it was reported, by between 3,500 and 4,000 guests.

He seems to have been a well-grounded person, very self-aware, not allowing the knighthood to go to his head. In the manuscript mentioned above, this is how he describes himself, during his time as a city councillor – in mock biblical language:

1. Now a certain man lived in that city and his name was John

2. And the height of him was not great, being but one cubit and a half.

3. Though he was small, he was puffed up, so that he waxed exceedingly proud, and he said, I am one of the great ones of that city.

The two Barringtons seem to have been seriously addicted to acquiring large boats. In 1879/80 Sir John owned *Minna*, a 20 ton, 58 foot yawl. In 1881 Lloyds show him as owning both *Minna* and *Belle*, a 37 ton, 70 foot schooner; likewise in 1882. In 1883 *Minna* had been sold to Belfast, Barrington holding on to *Belle* until he acquired

Foam in 1886, a 16 ton, 48 foot cutter. On John's death in May 1887, *Foam* passed to Charles, who retained her until 1892, when he returned her to John's son, John H. Barrington.

In 1892, Charles acquired the substantial *White Rose*, yawl-rigged, 58 feet long and weighing 42 tons. The previous owner had been Robert Browne MD, one of the Brown family of Brown Thomas's. She was a sturdy, roomy craft, substantial enough to cruise as far as St. Petersburg. Barrington, in July 1894, raced her in the Dalkey Regatta. This was quite a major sailing and social occasion in Dublin Bay, with throngs of fashionably attired ladies in attendance and bands of the Duke of Cornwall's Light Infantry and the North Staffordshire Regiment playing on the lawn of Sorrento House, the regatta shore centre.

Racing in some of the big boats competing in that event was not for the faint-hearted. Dr. O'Flaherty, in *Daffodil*, dropped his spinnaker boom on top of the unfortunate mark boat and had to retire. *Eurynone* and *Girotte* became entangled during a mark rounding incident – *Girotte*'s bowsprit fouling *Eurynone*'s topping lift. 'They waltzed for a few minutes together,' said the *Yachting World* report, before drifting apart. Barrington, in his 58 foot *White Rose,* sensibly kept away from these shenanigans and finished without incident.

White Rose had not been quite so lucky on June of that year when she went aground on a rock near Dalkey which the *Daily Independent* identified as the 'K; Byrne'. The name would not be familiar to current Dublin Bay sailors but apparently was a well-known hazard at the time. The scene was dramatic in the extreme, *White Rose* listing 40 degrees with a portion of her keel exposed. There was a large party on board, including some ladies. They were all brought ashore safely and presumably *White Rose* floated free with the rising tide.

There was another incident that autumn, on a fine Saturday afternoon, when *White Rose* and probably most of the boats on the station went fishing for mackerel. When the wind dropped, *White Rose* 'was taken by the strong flood tide on to the outside of the West Pier', says a report in one of the yachting journals, 'and her bottom became a regular *crasher* against the rocks which compose the breakwater.' Barrington was unhurt.

Among those fishing on that occasion, and very successfully, too, was an 'Eastern Potentate' and his 'cohort of young ladies'. You might wonder which of the royal clubs on that occasion had accommodated this unusual visitor and his cohort. The RSGYC? Hardly, given the upset caused some years previously by the visit of a man of the cloth who was not a member. Or, the RIYC, the committee of which became jittery when lady visitors refused to keep to their allotted spot on the club balcony? Or, was it the Absolute Club, whose owner was as cheerfully indifferent to the concerns of Alpine guides as he was to the sensibilities of his Quaker kinsfolk?

In 1896 another seminal figure in the history of the club appears among the boat owners in Kingstown: William Cotton. The family were for many years involved in the gas industry, William eventually becoming managing director of the Alliance and Dublin Gas Co, where his three sons also occupied senior positions. He was obviously well regarded in business circles, his directorships including the Dublin United Tramway Co., the Gas Meter Co. of London, and the Hibernian Bank. He was also co-founder and chairman of the Hibernian Insurance Co.

Cotton was also a director of Alex Findlater and Co. A Mr A. Findlater, it will be recalled, was in attendance on that historic day in April 1870, when Lord Longford had laid the first stone. The Findlater name recurs frequently over the years in the minutes of the Edward Yacht Club, the last occasion being for the 1942 annual general meeting, when a vote of sympathy was passed with the family of William Findlater, 'many years a member'.

William Cotton was also a politician, on the Irish parliamentary party side. He was an alderman (1899-1917) of Dublin Corporation and served as chairman of many corporation committees. He was elected Lord Mayor in 1911. He was elected as an MP for South County Dublin in December 1910 and held the seat until his death in 1917.

Alderman William Cotton.

Cotton's link with Barrington is first recorded in 1896 when Barrington sold (or transferred) the *White Rose* to Cotton, who retained the vessel until he died. Barrington, since 1895, following the example of his brother John, had had two boats at this time; the *White Rose*, and a 50 ton, 77 foot schooner called *Avalanche*. An odd name for a boat to be owned by a mountaineer, you might think, given that an avalanche had nearly done for Barrington and his guides when they were coming off the Eiger. But that's how the vessel was named when he acquired her from W.I. Doherty, his centre-city neighbour, a solicitor, who worked most conveniently around the corner at 61 Lower Dominick Street.

Charles Barrington died at his home, 18 Earlsfort Terrace, on 20 April 1901. He was buried in Mount Jerome rather than at the Friends' cemetery at Temple Hill or the Barrington family private vault at Glendruid, Brennanstown Road. Interestingly, the huge throng of mourners at his funeral include people who were afterwards recorded as members of the Edward Club, which would suggest that the then-membership of the Absolute Club just continued on to become members of the club under its new title and ownership status.

These included William Neville Stewart, H.M. Leask, J. Knox Foote, H. Moffitt, J.R. O'Connell, Herbert Jones, G.H. Locking, H. Willington, and John Lloyd (later, for thirteen years, Hon. Secretary of the Edward Yacht Club and then Hon. Treasurer for eight years after it had become the National Yacht Club).

Side View of clubhouse, with boat drying on gridiron. Absolute Club period.
(Lawrence Collection, National Library of Ireland)

7.

The Edward Club's Early Members

From a cartoon by Thomas Ryan, RHA

Kingstown Harbour is under control independent and absolutely indifferent to the elected authority of the township. The Harbour Commissioners are three inconsequential nobodies who on occasions are seen here, bedizened in cocked hats and gold lace. Their secretary is a person whose chief qualification for the position is not a transcendental knowledge of marine works and their care but a facility for fiddling and organ-blowing.

The fifth individual who exercises autocratic sway in certain harbour concerns, struts much on our town front, with the apparent object of airing his supercilious contempt for the mere Irish, when not indulging his snobbery by billiard playing within exclusive walls. – *Kingstown Echo*, September 1904

After the horrors of the Great War, many looked back on the two decades that preceded it as a sort of golden age. The Kingstown of the era (so charmingly evoked in Mary Hamilton's memoir *Green and Gold)* would seem to conform to this nostalgic narrative. It was a world of 'handsome terraces, interspersed with large houses surrounding quiet, shady parks, private to these residences where children played on smooth mown grass while their nurses did needlework for their charge'. Easter parades of fashionable ladies took place on the East Pier, and military bands performed on the bandstand – a mode of life very remote from the Ireland outside where there were already intimations of the revolutionary torrent that would sweep it all away.

It had a large cohort of comfortably retired people, attended to by a respectful servant class who, according to one calculation, constituted one-eighth of the township's population. To people of a certain age, the climate was believed to be especially kind, being – someone had worked it out – one or two degrees warmer than elsewhere on the island. Mary Hamilton mentioned particularly the women, lively intelligent old ladies who discussed art and music and who went to concerts of the Royal Dublin Society. Sons, nephews, grandsons, came to visit them from all parts of the Empire, from Quetta and Peshawar, from Cape Town and Bulawayo, from Calgary and Melbourne and Wellington. They knew all about the Royal Family, with ramifications and relationships at their fingertips.

Not surprisingly, then, when the promoters of the club took it over from the estate of Charles Barrington, they would have had little trouble with a title. There was probably a surge of monarchical euphoria at the time. The old queen was recently dead and the Edward VII had ascended the throne. Calling it the Edward Club probably looked like a good idea – after all, in displays of loyalty to the Crown, the other two Kingstown clubs had the advantage of 'Royal' in their titles. Thus using 'Edward' in the title neatly addressed whatever loyalist deficit members of the Club might have been conscious of.

The Articles of Agreement setting up the club under its new name have not survived but there is a memorial in the Registry of Deeds detailing the transfer of the clubhouse and effects from the Barrington estate to the trustees of the Edward Yacht Club dated 28 October 1901. The trustees were named as William Edmund O'Reilly Hamilton, William Francis Cotton and William Neville Stewart. Cotton has already been mentioned in the previous chapter; Hamilton, when he married Margaret Jane Taggert in 1887, described himself as 'Gentleman'. He lived at 8 De Vesci Terrace. Like many of the early club members his family had military connections – his father was a captain in the 39th (Dorsetshire) regiment He was appointed Secretary to the Irish board of Arthur Guinness on 1 September 1902. He died on 5 May 1911.

William Neville Stewart, the third trustee seems to have been the liveliest. Like Hamilton, he lived at De Vesci Terrace (No.2). Stewart sailed a 40 foot, nine ton cutter called *Lansquenet*. He had a job, described as 'travelling agent' with the Land Commission, in the department which dealt with church property. He was elected Hon. Secretary on 24 September 1904.

Pressed to remain in office the following year, he made what surely has to be one of the most self-effacing speeches ever made to a club meeting. It was 'hard lines', he said, that they should have to put up with him for a longer time. He feared he was inclined to leave the work he had to do to others and, in fact, he did not exert himself in the interest of the club in any way 'except to try to keep the peace'.

If the members were prepared to overlook his shortcomings he might remain a little longer solely so that they did not lose the services of their Hon. Treasurer, Mr. Berry, who, he said, had proved to be the ideal man for the job. The meeting wasn't buying any of this – which, judging by the minutes was largely untrue, anyway – and insisted on both men staying in their positions. The next year, cannily, he didn't attend but sent his resignation in writing.

In those years, before they got down to having a commodore, members didn't have a regular chairman for their meetings but elected one on an *ad hoc* basis. Stewart chaired the meeting of 5 October 1907. He died suddenly, just two months later on 4 December.

Trustees and their responsibilities concerned members in those years much more than they do now. About thirty years after the events of this period, the Dublin *Evening Herald*, on 14 May 1932, published an article which touched briefly on the club's early history. Regarding trustees it reads: 'It is worthy of note that the two trustees were the late Alderman W.F. Cotton and Mr. (now Rev. Sir John) O'Connell.'

On the face of it, this seems to conflict with the deed of transfer mentioned above – which has no mention whatever of O'Connell – but there is an explanation: there were in fact two sets of trustees, one for the premises, and the other for the debenture holders.

Just like their predecessors in 1870, the officers of the Edward Club had to have recourse to the debenture mechanism to fund the acquisition of the clubhouse and its assets from the Barrington estate. It worked the same way as the earlier mechanism, raffles being held from time to time to redeem the debentures or when a member died. O'Connell was, indeed, a major holder of these club debentures – as the minutes confirm – and also a trustee for the debenture holders.

Who was he, this reverend gentleman, who was a knight of the realm as well as a trustee and an active member of the Edward Yacht Club? Sir (Rev) John O'Connell was in fact another of these extraordinary people who feature from time to time in the club's history. An eminent figure in the legal profession, he was at various times Vice-President of the Incorporated Law Society, a director of the National Bank, a member of both the senate of Dublin University and the governing body of UCC, a member of the Royal Irish Academy, a fellow of the Royal Society of Antiquaries of Ireland, and Vice-President of the Statistical and Social Inquiry Society of Ireland.

He was the author of many pamphlets on social, religious and political matters; one of them, interestingly, was entitled 'Some considerations in reference to the establishment of an office of a public trustee in Ireland'. The National Library has his eyewitness description of the Easter Rising which he sent to Cecil Harmsworth, the newspaper proprietor. Harry Clarke, the stained glass artist, was a friend.

When his wife Mary, daughter of Thomas Scally of Deepwell in Blackrock, died in 1925 he entered the Benedictines at Downside but was ordained a secular priest in 1929 and served as a curate at St. Patrick's church in Soho. Pope Pius XI made him a knight of the Grand Cross of the Holy Sepulchre for services to the work, mission and schools of the Latin patriarchate in Palestine and Transjordan. His abandonment of a successful professional career in favour of a life as a humble curate caught the attention of the American press and resulted in some articles which can hardly have been welcomed by a man embracing a life of reticence and humility.

If any of O'Connell's achievements is worthy of remembrance today, it is surely his oversight of the construction of the Honan Collegiate Chapel in Cork. (Executor of Isabella Honan's will, he had discretion to direct the Honan estate to undefined charitable purposes.) This coherent blend of Hiberno-Byzantine styles with art nouveau and symbolist elements owes much to O'Connell's scholarship. His library, sold after his renunciation of club land and the world of sociology, academe and the law, included books on history, art, poetry, memoirs, belles-letters, Irish and theological literature and ancient maps of Ireland. The Honan chapel, incidentally, was one of the early major projects of the building firm, John Sisk & Co.

An auditor who refused to sign the 1908 accounts caused some upset at the 1909 Annual General Meeting on 25 September 1909. The problem was not so much the finances – there was 'a little profit', it appeared later – but the 'interests' of debenture holders and their relationship with the Club's Articles of Association, which he considered 'vaguely defined'. He advised that they seek counsel's opinion on the matter. O'Connell, the largest debenture-holder, was away when the then-chairman, Mr. Hickey, wished to talk to him about a submission to counsel, but eventually this took place and they were able to learn some unpleasant news from a Mr. Littledale, KC.

Honan Chapel, Cork
(courtesy wikipedia commons)

This they shared with a meeting of the debenture-holders, which took place on 30 October (48 of the debenture-holders were not members of the Club). Mr. Littledale had not yet put it in writing but his words nevertheless were pretty stark: 'they were clearly labouring under a misapprehension in considering they were a members' club as in reality the so-called debenture holders were shareholders running the club for their own profit and loss'.

This was not, of course, what they were about – shades of Captain Peacocke and Charles Barrington must have been hovering – and steps were immediately taken to have things put right. Unfortunately, documentation of the period has not survived that would explain clearly the ins and outs of the subsequent discussions. At any rate, over the winter of 1909-1910 the issue was resolved and a new deed, drafted by Littledale, conforming to the Articles of Association, was drawn up and, at a meeting on 25 June 1910, agreed to by both members and debenture holders. The matter didn't quite end there and it wasn't until 1912 that O'Connell was able to report that the new trust deed was about to be finalised. That seems to have satisfied everyone and the subject does not reappear in the minutes of subsequent club meetings.

John O'Connell seems to have played a decisive role in in all these discussions. The minutes suggest that his views were listened to with considerable respect by all parties – as indeed they well might; the US newspaper, the *St. Louis Despatch* asserted that as the country's leading solicitor he could command fees of up $500,000 a year, an enormous sum for the early 1900s.

In their outlook and way of life members of the club would not have differed much, if at all, from their counterparts in other clubs. (In fact, dual, and sometimes, triple membership of the waterfront clubs persisted up to our own times.) Unlike the Royal St. George, members of the landed family hardly feature, if at all, in the lists of those attending meetings of the Edward club. An exception was a Mr. G.H. Studdert, who was probably one of the Studderts of Bunratty Castle, a marriage connection of Dr. O'Flaherty, whose father, Jerome, had married Elizabeth Studdert in March 1848. Another was a Mr. Grubb, assistant Hon. Secretary for a time whose family connections occupy *twelve* pages of *Burke's Family Records.*

Doctors, in the early years, seem to have gravitated towards the Edward Yacht Club. Besides the inevitable Dr. R.G. O'Flaherty (participating in its activities in all its various guises ever since its first meeting back in 1869), members of the profession attending meetings included Doctors Carnegie, Connolly, Fitzgibbon, Norton, Dowdall and Hadden. There were two Scotts who were probably doctors, one of them, Dr Burnett Scott, served later on the club committee and as a flag-officer in the 1930s. A Dr. George Dampier-Bennett does not seem to have attended club meetings; he was an eminent medical figure, author of several works on medical matters. Besides the Edward Club, according to E. McDowel Cosgrave's *Dublin and County Dublin in the 20th Century*, he was a member also of the Kingstown Rifles Club and the Royal Albert. Octavius Studdert Maunsell was another doctor who frequently appeared at club meetings. A Boer War veteran, he had a considerable medical and army curriculum vitae.

Another calling that seems to have gravitated towards the new club was the military one. There was a belief that the army men who joined the club felt more comfortable there than in the Royal Irish Yacht Club which had a strong Quaker component and therefore could be expected to think less kindly of people involved in the military. This is undoubtedly a waterfront myth; soldiers and naval officers feature among the RIYC membership and there is no suggestion that they were anything but valued members.

Still, it's curious that the minutes of the Edward Club that survived the fires include among those attending one particular meeting a General Kelly, Colonels Kelly and Parker as well as Captains Brown and Graves. Participating at later meetings were a Captain Birt, a Captain Manders and a Major Newenham, who was a country member.

This military strain persisted up to the 1930s; one committee had among its members two Major Wallers, James and Edgar, members of the many-branched Waller family whose pedigree occupies twelve full pages of *Burke's Irish Family Records*. A Colonel Loftus Bryan was an early member when it was the Edward Yacht Club; years later, in 1931, he was recorded as arguing about the mode of electing new members alongside a Cumann na nGaedheal T.D., Batt O'Connor (who in 1919-1922 had belonged to a another kind of army).

Racing in Dublin Bay at this time – like today – was very much left on an all-club basis to Dublin Bay Sailing Club. Apart from their own biannual regattas, the waterfront clubs had not to concern themselves with the chores of race management. The Edward had its first club regatta in 1907. Some Edward men were racing with DBSC before the change over from the Absolute Club and, indeed, probably raced from it.

Besides Dr. O'Flaherty, they included W.B. Stuart, G. Alcorn, H. Martyn Leask, Cons. Barker, Dr. Carnegie, Henry Falkner, W. Findlater, R. Lloyd and David Turner. A Mr. Brown was turned down for DBSC membership in August 1891, presumably because he quoted only the Absolute Club as his address. John Adair Magauran, afterwards a long-serving Hon. Secretary of DBSC, was an early member of the Edward (he later served on the Edward committee).

The phrase 'billiard-playing within exclusive walls' in that diatribe against the unfortunate Harbour Commissioners (see title page above) refers, of course to a waterfront club. Whether this might apply to the Edward Club is anyone's guess. Exclusive the club certainly was, to a degree. The final paragraph in the 1932 *Herald* article reads:

> From its inauguration the Edward Yacht Club was extremely progressive if also somewhat exclusive. It never sought members but the only qualification demanded of those who became candidates … for membership was that they should be gentlemen in the broad and proper sense of the term, and sportsmen.

Few club members of the time, one imagines, would have disagreed with that opinion.

8.

The Edward Club – Ebb and Flows, 1901-1931

The general meeting of 1931 is a good vantage point from which to look back on how the club had fared since the regime change of 1901. Not at all badly, you would think, looking through the club's minutes of that period, the twilight years of the *ancien régime*. The minutes, terse, almost laconic, are sparing in their details of what was happening on the ground (or, in this case, on the water.) Nor do newspaper or law court reports add very much; the new men, industrious, prosaic types, were not the people to attract public interest.

However the minutes do show that in the early periods there were worries about the club's finances, caused in the main by the state of the clubhouse, which after the Barrington regime, was hardly in a state you would expect of a gentlemen's club. The Chairman, William Neville Stewart, at a general meeting on 21 February 1904, stated the situation frankly. There had been a large outlay incurred after the purchase of the club in putting the premises in proper repair, and the committee had made a number of improvements within the building to provide for the comfort and convenience of the members, such as the purchase of a new billiard table. All would move along smoothly, he thought, if only members were to take up unissued debentures.

Action was promptly taken. Four members, on the spot, agreed to take up unissued debentures and there was talk about issuing a circular to other members who, up to this, had not done so. What seems to have resolved the immediate problem, however, was that was the Committee took a sharpish look at expenses and cut down on all unnecessary expenditure.

Austerity seems to have worked for a while and at the 1906 October meeting the Chairman was able to congratulate the members on the 'satisfactory state of their club'. Dr. Scott and a Mr. Davis still had misgivings about the level of expenses. This was countered by the Chairman saying that the committee for some time had been considering a scheme to bring them under control; he wanted a small sub-committee to meet the members to discuss future management of the club. Details are scanty but what seems to be happening here is the establishment of the club's first finance committee.

Looking back with our perspective it's extraordinary, how relatively small, in those years, was the club's actual membership. In September 1910, full members (so-called 'resident members'), each paying the full annual subscription of £3, numbered 88. Country members, paying £1 per annum, totalled 50. Proposals that each member seek to introduce a new member were never acted upon, which would suggest that no one was bothered overmuch about the membership level.

It's a wonder that with so low a base the club didn't go the same way it had in previous years. Social activity in the club must have been intense. At one meeting a Mr. Peter (probably R.M. Peter, of 11 Clarinda Park West) gave 'some interesting statistics as to the consumption of whiskey and the attendance of members'. Tantalizingly, no details were given as to what *that* was about. There was a call at one meeting for the price of whiskey to be reduced to sixpence a glass. At the same meeting someone asked who had checked the stock in the cellars. Told it was the assistant-secretary (the respectable Mr. Grubb), he judged this 'satisfactory'.

Details of club opening hours would not appear in the minutes. However, a special meeting on 4 January 1913 decreed that in the winter months the club was to close at *12:30 am*. What was going on in the club during the summer months, after that hour, you might justifiably wonder.

It was card playing no doubt – one of the rooms was designated as the card room and bridge was a popular pastime, with many outsiders participating. So much so that in the autumn of 1908 there was an outbreak of hair-splitting, trying to designate the precise status of visitors participating in bridge tournaments. Were they honorary members 'during the tournament' or honorary members 'only during the time they were engaged in the tournament'. The latter designation, proposed by Dr. O'Flaherty, was the one that found favour at a special meeting held on 31 October to decide to decide the issue.

Was this a desire to keep up standards, perhaps, or a signal making it clear that the club's primary function was providing for yachtsmen not card players? The Dublin Bay racing routine was well-established by this time. Many members of the Edward Club were also members of Dublin Bay Sailing Club which, as mentioned earlier, drew its membership from all of the waterfront clubs.

There was O'Flaherty himself, of course, plus Henry Martyn Leask, John Knox Foote, C.V. Lowry, Dr Charles Burnett Scott, Sydney Orr, Robert Caldwell, Henry Falkner, John Adair Magauran, C.I. Moore and A.N. Sumerling (grandfather of Michael Halpenny). Others would not be identifiable because they didn't turn up at the Edward Club's six-monthly meetings.

Keeping up with the other two clubs in this period, the Edward at its meeting on 26 September 1908 agreed to welcome:

> All the members of the Royal Family visiting Ireland, the Lord Lieutenant and their personal staff in attendance, the Chief Secretary, the Commander of the forces, all naval officers on the active list visiting Kingstown.

This was proposed by Dr Burnett Scott, his colleague Dr. O'Flaherty presiding. Army, naval and Royal Irish Constabulary were also included.

Edward Club's members had busy social lives with interesting pastimes other than racing boats in Dublin Bay. Both Martyn Leask and Knox Foote were members of musical societies and their names appear in reports of concerts and musical events. It was very much like the world portrayed in Joyce's *Dubliners*. Sealy Jeffares was another Edward Club member who was part of the Dublin musical scene. His amusing songs such as 'I wear her portrait next to my heart' were much appreciated.

Martyn Leask and Knox Foote were on the Dublin Castle visiting list and attended many of the grand social events of the day. Both had military titles – initially Lieutenant, later Captain – by virtue of their membership of a volunteer battalion of the Royal Welch Fusiliers. Martyn Leech was a Water Wag sailor, occasionally acting as Officer of the Day for Wag races.

Finances continued to be healthy until well into the Great War period. In his report to the annual general meeting on 8 August 1914 – the week the war broke out – the auditor, J.A. Kinnear, referred to the 'prosperous state of the Club'. This prompted some members, in a surge of benevolence, to propose that the bonus of the house steward, George Wilton, be increased from £10 to £20, but the chairman, Burnett Scott, was having none of it and called them sharply to order.

The club's 'prosperous' balance sheet was again mentioned at the 1915 annual general meeting on 21 August, with congratulations all round for what had been achieved 'in spite of many difficulties from which the club suffered from the present war'. These would have included a ban on yachting in the Bay, imposed by the station naval commander, Admiral le Marchant.

It wasn't always observed. Miss Florence Blacker Douglas, who owned the Dublin Bay Twenty One Footer, *Estelle*, once went out for a sail and struck a German U-boat, lying hidden on the sea-bed. Or so family lore has it. An aged retainer, looking over the side, lost his false teeth in the excitement. Perhaps the ban wasn't too strictly enforced or else Admiral le Marchant was disinclined to take on Miss Florence Blacker Douglas.

Double-ended Water Wag, being attended to at the boathouse, then situated in what is now the car-parking area in front of the club.

At any rate, the ban could not have but affected club finances, although in the 1916 minutes of meetings held on 10 June there are no references to finances – nor indeed to the effects of the Easter Rising (nor, for that matter, to the war). What, on the other hand, greatly concerned some 37 members was the oligarchical rule of the committee which had been in office unchanged since 1912. They requisitioned a special general meeting demanding that three members of the Committee to retire each year. Their motion failed to reach the required majority and so Dr. Charles Burnett Scott, Henry Falkner, W.T Mackay, H. Moffett (Hon. Secretary), William

B. Stuart (Hon. Treasurer), S.W. Nugent and C.D. Harris continued to remain in office – although Harris retired later.

By 1917, the effects of the war were having effect. Sydney Orr, at a general meeting held on 15 September, suggested a voluntary increase of 10/- in the annual subscription to reduce the deficit (amount unstated). Other members were prepared to pay more. A lone voice was that of George Arthur Newsom who thought the solution was not increasing fees but acquiring more members. Newsom was an important figure in the business world, a director of Jacobs, the biscuit firm, and played a very active and constructive role in the club's affairs until his death on 27 June 1933. (DBSC still commemorates his memory each year at its prize giving by awarding the Newsom Cup for the best one-design boat.)

Finally, at a general meeting held on 28 September 1918 the members reluctantly agreed that they would have to increase the membership fee from £3 to four guineas. An entry fee was not considered a good idea up to this point and indeed, at the 1919 AGM, it was explicitly ruled out of discussion until 'club membership more nearly approached one hundred members'.

This duly happened and an extraordinary general meeting on 24 January 1920 imposed, after some argument, an entry fee of three guineas. Also at the 1920 meeting, William M. Stuart broached what must long have been the then equivalent of the elephant in the room – the election of flag-officers, which, of course, would include a commodore.

Early committees seems to have slow off the mark in acquiring noble patronage (or else their efforts were rebuffed by whoever might have been approached.) The custom of having an eminent personage at the head of yacht clubs was very prevalent across the channel and, indeed, elsewhere. So much so that for the club and its predecessors not to have a noble patron at its head for many years seems almost perverse.

In fact, since Lord Longford's time, there was no eminent patron of the club until a special general meeting on 29 October 1921 when the Earl of Pembroke was elected Commodore.

Why Reginald Herbert, 15th Earl of Pembroke and 12th Earl of Montgomery was chosen is not stated. The War of Independence was coming to a close at the time and it seems equally perverse, when the club had managed to do without one for years, to elect as Commodore, at this particular juncture, a prominent member of the British establishment. True, large swathes of the southern part of the city were part of the Pembroke estate, but the Earl of Pembroke's s personal connections with Ireland were few. He remained Commodore until 1931.

The club's first Vice-Commodore was George Arthur Newsom, elected in 1921, who with his elegant signature signed off most of the minutes up to the change of regime in 1931. Henry Falkner was the club's first Rear-Commodore and he remained in that positon until 1924 when Dr. Burnett Scott took over. Scott remained in that role and was active in the position until well after the 1931/2 change of regime.

The Dún Laoghaire yacht clubs, based in what many of their members still called Kingstown, was not totally immune to the political turmoil persisting elsewhere. One Sunday night, in late October 1926, an attempt was made to destroy by explosives the flag staffs of the three clubs. The motive suggested in the press was during recent months the clubs' ensigns, each of which contained the Union Jack in one quarter, had been flown from the flag staffs. For some time after the establishment of the State no flags were displayed, but with the return of more settled conditions committees apparently thought that the ensigns could be safely brought out.

The names of members attending general meetings in the early part of the decade don't reflect much of a post-war change. The names of earlier members such as S.M. Nugent, A.N. Sumerling, John Adair Magauran, W.B. Stuart and R. Caldwell continued to appear, though that of Captain Henry Martyn Leask is not among them. He had died on 15 December 1918 and is buried in Deans Grange cemetery. He was born in Lanarkshire, Scotland. His business, H.M. Leask & Co, located at 14-16 Sir John Rogerson's

Quay, was described in an advertisement as 'manufacturers of pure linseed cake, linseed meal and crushed linseeds'.

The name of Francis Arthur Marrable does not reappear either as he had died on 15 August 1915 fighting with the 7th battalion of the Royal Dublin Fusiliers. Herbert Snowden Findlater, also of the 7th battalion, died in action a few days later. It's not clear whether he was an actual Edward Club member but the Findlater family name occurs in the records from the club's early days, and indeed a Mr. A. Findlater was among the official party at the laying of the first stone in April 1870. The 7th was one of the 'Pals Battalions' established to encourage recruitment by drawing on men of the same neighbourhood or vocational background. It was in action in August 1915 in Suvla Bay, Gallipoli.

John Knox Foote certainly appeared post-war. He was now Captain Knox Foote, making sure his presence was noted, perhaps, by frequently moving votes of thanks to the officers and committee at the end of meetings. He served for a time on the committee. For Foote and Sealy Jeffares, those cheerful evenings performing at musical concerts seemed to be a thing of the past.

Dr Richard O'Flaherty's name does not reappear in the post-war minutes either. He had died on 15 February 1913, leaving, for the time, the not inconsiderable sum of £20,078.

The sense you get of the club's activities at this period is not a dullness exactly but a certain sameness, a lack of variety, a disinclination to adapt to the mood of the times, exemplified by members' reaction to a proposal in December 1923 to hold a dance in the boathouse. 'It caused,' notes the minutes, 'considerable discussion', which terminated with a decision to grant permission with the following proviso:

> Provided that the dance committee form a guarantee fund so that in case of loss no financial liability will fall upon the club funds and also, on the occasion of a dance, the club reading room, card-room and billiard-room be reserved for the members.

Not an unreasonable stipulation, you might say, and very much in accord with the waterfront clubs' unwillingness at the time to have women near their usual haunts. Another entry, in the minutes of a meeting on 28 September 1928, shows a softening of attitude but reads strangely:

> On 1st May to the 30th September during the summer months ladies accompanied by a member may be entertained up to 10pm. Only the coffee room, the boat-house and *the roof* shall be available for such guests.

After the turmoil and tribulations of the previous decade, with friends dead or departed, dull routine may have had its attractions for members of the Edward Club. A game of billiards, a game of cards, a drink with friends, varied with a DBSC race on Saturdays – many would be happy to settle for just that.

9.

The Granard Years

Bernard Arthur William Patrick Hastings Forbes,
8th Earl of Granard. KP, GCVO (1874-1948)
Commodore, National Yacht Club, 1931-1941

The 1930s was the decade when the members of the Edward Yacht Club turned away from the received ways of doing things and fixed their gaze, with some degree of uncertainty, on a changing world.

The first acknowledgement of changing times was amending the club's name from the Edward Yacht Club to the National Yacht Club. Club lore has it that it was promoted by the Earl of Granard and a committee of members meeting with the trustees and asking for the change. However, the club minutes, recording the event, are almost off-hand about it and not preceded by suggestion of any earlier discussion. It all happened, without preamble, at an

Extraordinary General Meeting held on 7 March 1931. The minutes read as follows:

> The following resolutions were proposed and unanimously passed:
>
> Rule 4. To suspend entrance fee to the 30th June 1931 retrospectively.
>
> 2 To change the name of the Club to the National Yacht Club, adopt new ensign (Royal blue with gold harp), alter financial year to the 31sr March, adjust other dates in connection with the alteration.
>
> These alterations were proposed by J.S. McIntyre and seconded by G.R. O'Connor. Messrs Mackay, Duncan and Colonel Loftus Bryan also spoke.

The meeting was chaired by the Vice-Commodore, George Arthur Newsom. Those in attendance included long-time members Studdert, Foote, Magauran, Maunsell, Scott, O'Hanlon, Turner, Neale, Ingram and Duncan.

The change of the club's title and the election of the Earl of Granard as Commodore was celebrated by what seems to have been a particularly enjoyable *At Home* on 19 July 1931. A musical entertainment was provided by members and friends; they included Captain Turner and, not unexpectedly, Mr. Sealy Jeffares.

Prominent guests included Her Excellency, Mrs. McNeill, wife of the Governor-General, as well as members of the Cabinet: Minister for Finance Ernest Blythe and Mrs. Blythe, the Minister for Local Government and Mrs. Mulcahy, the Minister for Lands and Fisheries and Mrs. Lynch and the Minister for Education and Mrs. O'Sullivan.

Also among the attendance was the Chief Justice and Mrs. Kennedy, General and Mrs. McMahon, Major-General and Mrs. Brennan, Major-General and Mrs. McNeill, Major-General and Mrs. Sweeney, General W.R.E. Murphy, Deputy Commissioner S. Coogan, the Rt. Rev. Mons. Walsh, P.P., VG, the Rev. Canon and Mrs. Chamberlain, the Rev. Canon and Mrs. Pim, Major Cotter, Mr.

and Mrs. Herbert Dudgeon, Mr. and Mrs. J.P. Stephens, Sir Thomas
and Lady Robinson, Capt. A.F. Holmes, R.N. and Mrs. Holmes, Mr
and Mrs. C. McGloughlin, Mr. J.J. Halpin, President of the Chamber
of Commerce and Mrs Halpin.

Why there should be such an eminent assembly present on the
occasion of the re-naming of a yacht club is a bit curious, a little over
the top even. And in presenting the Commodore's flag – enclosed in
an inscribed silver casket – to the Earl of Grenard, Mr. P.J. Lawrence,
the Vice-Commodore, made remarks which are not particularly
enlightening:

> It was their desire that in the realms of sport the Club should
> uphold its name as national in their country. When visiting
> yachts arrived at Dún Laoghaire, they, as the National Yacht
> Club, would feel it incumbent upon them to extend fitting
> courtesy to their visitors and they meant to do it.

As though the Dún Laoghaire clubs did not already welcome
visiting yachts?

The slightly odd note struck by the speeches, as well as the attendance of such eminent members of the cabinet and officers of
state, would, at this remove, prompt suspicion. Had there been
something in the background about which no one at the time was
prepared to talk about publicly? Such as what perhaps might be
raised by a curious note which recently came to light in the club
records. It was from Brendan Ebrill, a long-time member and for
eight years the Hon. Secretary of Dublin Bay Sailing Club:

> To: The Commodore, National Yacht Club.
>
> To-day I had a chat with Vincent McAllister and he told me
> of the background to the change of our Club's name from the
> 'Edward' to the 'National'. I had not known this and I was
> intrigued.
>
> I suggest that it should be printed in Mainsheet before it is
> forgotten. Perhaps if you cannot persuade Vincent go into
> print, you may persuade someone to ghost the story for him.

BRIEF SYNOPSIS

In 1922 our new Free State government was in constant communication with the British government concerning the details of the handover of functions etc.

In those (pre Aer Lingus days) the officials arrived and departed via Dún Laoghaire (Kingstown).

The President of the Executive Council was Mr. W.T. Cosgrave and he sought a premises close to the Mail Boat berth
where he could entertain delegates in more privacy than in
a hotel or suchlike. The Edward Y.C. was a suitable location
and accepted a proposal that it should be decorated and up-
dated at the expense of Mr. Cosgrave's government and be
available for his purposes. Somewhere in the doing of all this
the change of name was made.

With kind regards,

Yours sincerely, Brendan Ebrill

Brendan Ebrill and Vincent McAllister have long since gone to
their reward and the matter was not pursued any further. The Granard estate have been unable to help. The files in the Office of Public
Works in the National Archives contain no reference to any work
undertaken at the Edward Yacht Club. Nor do the club minutes
throw any light on the matter, which would not be surprising given
the fraught and indeed dangerous political situation at the time.

Some further light on this curious by-way of Irish history comes
from an extract from a letter from Dr. Alf Delany to Con Murphy
(date indistinct, probably when Con was Commodore, 2005-8):

In the mid-1920s or slightly later, the Free State government
needed a reception area for distinguished visitors arriving on
the mail boat. The Edward YC was in a poor shape at that
period and it was thought a National YC could take over the
club and fill the government requirement. The exact date I
am not sure of. Lord Granard (of Newtown Forbes), a senator and Commodore of the North Shannon YC, was the first
Commodore. A few Longford people, including my father

(Hon. Secretary, NSYC) were persuaded to become members. My father didn't keep up his membership.

His father, he adds, was the source of this information.

There is also, as pointed out earlier, the curious matter of the election as Commodore of the Earl of Pembroke at a special general meeting held on 29 October 1921. For a club that had not bothered to look for an aristocratic patron for forty years or more, it was a distinctly odd decision, especially right in the middle of the Anglo-Irish Treaty negotiations. A coincidence perhaps? But, with the lack of any further documentation the whole matter has to remain a tantalizing enigma.

On the change of name, there were also some interesting observations from *The Examiner* (20 July 1931):

> An increase of vitality for the Club and for yachting is promised - the old institution was dying of inanition. It was the creation of a regime that has passed and half pay was writ large over it. What has happened now is something more than a reconstitution. The Club has been democratised, or popularised, in fashion similar which has had such happy results in the case of the Royal Dublin Society.

A bit overly ambitious or somewhat premature? Many of the *ancien régime* (if you want to regard them that way) continued, after the change of name, to maintain their customary sway. Dr. Octavius Studdert Maunsell continued to attend and contribute to club meetings as he had done since he returned from the Boer War. So also did Col. Loftus Bryan, Captain Macraith, Captain Knox Foote, S.C. Studdert and Dr. Burnett Scott. John Lloyd continued as Hon. Treasurer (he had been Hon. Secretary for the previous thirteen years). In 1933, Sealy Jeffares became Hon. Secretary and finally, in 1939, despite pleadings of his fellow members, succeeded in resigning. This was the same Sealy Jeffares who, as we have seen, was something of a star on the amateur musical scene before the First World War and – it so turns out – a grand-uncle of Rupert Jeffares, a long-time Secretary-Manager of Howth Yacht Club.

Another NYC member, whose service in the British Navy during the first World War should, in theory, have attached him to the ancien régime, was Donal Joseph O'Sullivan, BL., at this period Clerk of the Senate of the Irish Free State. He was a member of the NYC committee in 1932. He was another of the extraordinary people who keep appearing in the Club's history. Born in Liverpool of Irish parents, he entered the British civil service as a first division clerk and during the war served as a naval signals officer on board a mine-sweeper on convoy escort duty. After returning to the civil service, he was transferred at his own request to Dublin.

Under his parents' influence, he had already acquired an early interest in Ireland. He learnt Irish at Gaelic League classes in London and during holidays at his grandparents' home in Kerry. His major interest was Irish folk music. Over his lifetime his many scholarly publications on the music and songs of Ireland had a major impact, contributed hugely to the revival of Irish music and influenced such artists as Sean O Riada and Paddy Moloney of the Chieftains.

The Clerk of the Senate, Donal O'Sullivan, adjusting the cap of the Earl of Granard, at the National Yacht Club's At Home, 19 July 1931. On the right is Mrs. Josephine McNeill, wife of the Governor-General.

O'Sullivan lectured on international affairs at TCD (1951-62) and on Irish folk music in UCD (1951-62). He was a life member of the Royal Irish Academy. His book *The Irish Free State and Its Senate* (1940) has been described as factual if 'tendentious' apologia for the Treatyite side. He served one term in Seanad Éireann (1943-4) having been elected on the cultural and educational panel.

In his sailing days, he and solicitor Arthur Cox shared a 36 foot sailing cruiser called *Bonnie Jean*. In September 1932, their cruising activities off Dunmore East caught the attention of the local correspondent of the *Examiner* to whom they described their delighted exploration of the Barrow the Nore and the Siúr. For this expedition they had dismantled the mast and sails which they had left at Dunmore East.

Politics and Irish folk music apart, he was a man of wide culture, extraordinarily well-read and, perhaps owing to his Senate position, enjoyed the company and conversation of some of the great figures of the era – Yeats, for one, Gogarty, AE Russell and, at least on one occasion, Michael Collins. He knew Paris as well as he knew Dublin. Reading of the death of Hitler, his thoughts were of the beautiful medieval German buildings wrecked during the war, such as Cologne Cathedral, 'one of the glories of Christendom standing gaunt and damaged amid a sea of rubble', and Ratisbon 'with its noble Gothic cathedral and its Church of St. James, built in the purest Byzantine style by Irish monks of the twelfth century.'

All this can be read in *The Spice of Life*, a collection of his essays which appeared originally in the *Times Pictorial* and re-published in 1948 by Browne and Nolan. There is little here about sailing, apart from a reference to bringing a new boat home from the Thames through the canals and rivers of southern England rather than round the coast. He knew Homer and the Greeks well; gazing one day at the faint ripples of a sunlit Kerry inlet he could recall a line from Aeschylus, 'the many-twinkling smile of ocean'.

This great scholar of Irish music was also very knowledgeable about the music hall. Hearing too many products of Tin Pan Alley at a bus queue, he mused on the possibility of setting up a Busker School, which would teach a more varied repertoire. (Not the work of Percy French though, a good friend, 'but his songs always seemed to me to be friendly caricatures rather than the real thing.') He was not optimistic about the future of the Irish language and disliked children being taught through Irish by non-native speakers. Yet he could write that, 'those who have the gift to acquire it (be their number large or small) will gain an intellectual treasure of a kind that, for an Irishman, exceeds any other and lasts a lifetime'.

Then there were the two Major Wallers who were members of the club committee in 1937, Major Edgar Waller and Major J.H. de Waller. Nothing at this stage is known of Major Edgar but, of the latter, quite a lot. In fact, to describe him as a typical member of the *ancien régime* with the usual military connections would diminish him somewhat. Major James Hardress de Warrenne Waller, DSO OBE was much more than that; he was one of the most gifted, visionary and versatile civil engineers of his generation. The military rank and Anglo-Irish lineage, professionally useful though it might have been, was largely an irrelevance in the context of his civil engineering and civic achievements. Jim Waller, as he was known to his friends, served as Rear-Commodore of the National for five years from 1934 to 1938 inclusive. (See Sidelines section).

The Earl of Granard or, to give him his full name and title, Bernard Arthur William Patrick Hastings Forbes, 8th Earl of Granard, at first glance would seem an unlikely agent of change. His career, for a member of the peerage with some good connections, would seem conventional enough: military service (South African war, then World War I) as well as an appointment at the Royal Household (Lord-in-Waiting), Assistant Postmaster-General, Master of the Horse, and Special Envoy to announce the accession of George V to various courts of Europe. Unusually, however, he was a Catholic, and his higher education was not at Oxford or Cambridge but privately, under the direct supervision of Cardinal Newman.

Unusually too for his class, he was a Home Ruler and politically a Liberal. A participant in the 1917 Irish Convention, he was a signatory to the report recording the views of most nationalist participants (but not those of Sinn Féin, who boycotted the Convention). Later, and in tune with the policy of the new rulers to accommodate representatives of the old regime within the Free State structures, he was appointed to Seanad Éireann. He spoke rarely and only in support of the Cosgrave Government. When Fianna Fáil came to power, he was again appointed to the Seanad, becoming a behind-the-scenes intermediary between Éamon de Valera and the British Government.

One of Granard's s own proposals at this time, sent to the Dominions Office, might be resurrected in one form or another if re-negotiation of the Six County constitutional position ever became a political possibility: the establishment of a joint north-south assembly, with representatives from the Dáil and Stormont, elected by proportional representation.

His views on de Valera are – to put it mildly – not particularly friendly; they were, coloured, perhaps, by his own civil war experiences. In February 1923 irregulars had attempted to demolish Castle Forbes, the Granard family home. They didn't make good fist of it. Two mines were planted in front of the house, only one of which went off. The frontage was damaged but there was no fire. The irregulars were either incompetent or else their hearts weren't in it. The action cannot have been popular locally. Granard was one of the few Irish landlords whose religious and political views – Catholic and nationalist – would have been in accord with those of his tenants. `

Granard was formally elected Commodore twelve months after the re-naming of the club. It happened at the annual general meeting, on 18 June 1932. (Seemingly, the election was to take place at the 1931 annual general meeting but perhaps arrangements had not been finalised in time.) Granard had not yet been officially recorded as Commodore when he was presented with the Commodore's flag. This is how the 1932 minutes read:

Election of Flag Officers and Committee:

Commodore - The Rt. Hon. Senator the Earl of Granard, K.P., G.C.V.O

Vice-Commodore - Mr. P.J. Lawrence

Rear-Commodore - Master O'Hanlon.

Proposed by Doctor Scott, seconded by Sealy Jeffares. Elected unanimously.

The election of Philip Lawrence as Vice-Commodore in 1931 had seemed extraordinary. He had never before served on the Committee nor had even attended any club meetings. He was a director of the Irish American Oil Company, and there was probably a connection to Granard in that the family of Granard's wife, the American heiress Beatrice Mills, had considerable oil interests. Lawrence served for two terms as Commodore before handing over to Master O'Hanlon. He didn't attend club meetings after that, but remained as trustee for some years. There is no record of his being involved in sailing.

Two of the honorary members elected on this occasion (and both were proposed and seconded by Scott and Jeffares) are of some interest: His Excellency, Governor-General James McNeill and Mr. William T. Cosgrave. The McNeill election, at this time, would have been straight forward enough; it was in conformity with a 1923 decision replacing the title 'Lord Lieutenant' with 'Governor-General' in the list of honorary members.

But the election of W.T. Cosgrave as an honorary member, a month after his government lost power, was certainly unusual at the time and, indeed, probably would have been so at any time. It was a period of extremely heated, and sometimes murderous, political debate. Not that there would have been much opposition to Cosgrave within the club. Membership included two Cumann na nGaedheal TDs, Batt O'Connor and James Walter Beckett, head of J. & W. Beckett, one of the leading building contracting firms in Dublin.

The Beckett family were involved with the club since 1923 at the earliest. Henry Herbert attended the annual general meeting on 18 September of that year. He was elected to the club committee in 1925 and again in 1926. He was an uncle of the writer Samuel Beckett. Another Beckett, Howard, was among the crew of a Ringsend sailing trawler which struck the rocks near the Irish Lights depot in Dún Laoghaire Harbour and sank during the great storm of 11-12 November 1915. (The Beckett building yard was in Ringsend which might explain his being aboard a vessel from that area.)

The *Wicklow People* reported:

> The crew of four, John Whelan, William Whelan, Howard Beckett and G. Sherlock were in grave danger, but eventually, through the efforts of the coastguards, were enabled to jump ashore close to the steps of the Yacht Club.

James Walter Beckett, the TD, raced a small cruiser, *Kitsune,* in DBSC races from 1928 until 1932. His selection as a Cumann na nGaedhael deputy was due not so much for his political opinions as for his business experience. He retired from DBSC racing in July 1932 and died in December 1938. His son David continued the Beckett family connection with sailing, racing a small 4-ton sloop named *Dara* in DBSC races in the 1970s, and in 1973 sailed her to Brittany for which he received the Irish Cruising Club Strangford Cup (no mean achievement in such a small vessel.

Kitsune was then passed on to David Ring, who lived at Pakenham Road. For David and his brother John it was not a happy acquisition. On 2 September 1934, returning from a Seapoint Sailing

Dara

Club race – which had been cancelled because of heavy weather – *Kitsune* was struck by a squall and foundered. Luckily for the Ring brothers, they were picked up by another yacht in the area, *Aleatha* (R. Hay), but the two other members of the crew, Robert Alexander Mitchell and Christopher Doyle, were lost.

Coming back to the subject of politics, George Arthur Newsom, at a meeting on 20 June 1931, tabled a motion barring discussions at club meetings of a political or polemical character, but he withdrew it when the Chairman, P.J. Lawrence, assured him that he would not 'as long as he occupied the chair of the club, permit, and would always rule out of order, anything in the nature of a political or polemical discussion.'

All manner of interpretation can be read nowadays into some of these changes. The removal of the reference to a royal personage in the club title, followed by the election of Granard as Commodore, is certainly curious – all the more so in that Granard would have been one of the very few people in all of Ireland who personally knew the royal personage in question. (The post-nominal GCVO – Grand Cross, Victorian Order – attached to the Granard title was for personal service to the Sovereign.) Curious, but given the paucity of record, will have to remain just so.

10.

⁰

Changing Times, 1931-1941

The condition of the clubhouse was something which had not
received adequate attention from earlier committees. From time
to time people complained; at the 1910 annual general meeting T.J.
Duncan (still a member, twenty years later) pointed out that the
clubhouse was in a dilapidated and dirty state and that the windows
were filthy. And at the 1913 AGM, it was announced that a member
had offered £20 to have the dining room papered and other sundry
improvements carried out. A circular was then issued asking members to subscribe as well. What response this got is not known.

The sad state of the clubhouse was only revealed later (in 1935)
when many of the deficiencies had been put right:

> ... the building was in a really dangerous condition owing to
> apparently total neglect for many years ... (requiring) point-
> ing the stone supporting pillars and cutting the rust off and
> tarring the iron pillar supports - roof repairs, repairing and
> in one case renewing windows which had suffered from
> years of exposure to the weather... installing several modern
> fireplaces in various rooms....re-covering the billiard-table,
> installing a large anthracite stove in the dining room which
> proved of inestimable value to the premises.... renewing of
> the window frame .and window and re-papering and deco-
> ration of the card-room , installing a proper bar-room, a tele-
> phone box .. and complete overhauling and, where necessary,
> renewing of the sanitary arrangements and the re-decorating

Aerial picture c. 1933 showing the National Yacht Club (left)
and Royal St. George Yacht Club (right)

and papering of the lavatory...also the exterior of the club
has been kept freshly painted.

Undoubtedly, money was a factor and the lean 1930s was not
the time to go looking for it. Yet somehow the necessary funding
did emerge, thanks in part to committee changes and a realisation
on everyone's part that the social attractions offered by the club
were simply inadequate – and something had to be done about it.

A paragraph in the final paragraph in the minutes of an EGM on
13 January 1934 puts the issue pretty clearly:

> It was the feeling of all present that the club could and should
> be made more amenable to present conditions of social life
> and be thus be an attraction and as asset to the members.

The major committee change at this stage was Thos. J. Hamilton,
who succeeded (after an interval of two years) George Arthur Newsom as Vice-Commodore. Newsom had been Vice-Commodore
since October 1921 and retired in May 1931. Newsom's immediate

successor in May 1931 was P.J. Lawrence, followed in 1933 by Master O'Hanlon. Hamilton took over the Vice-Commodore position in June 1934 and remained in that office until May 1941, when he became Commodore for the next two years (Granard had retired at that stage).

It was during Hamilton's tenure that the club's fortunes finally took a turn for the better. Perhaps Hamilton's business background may have helped. He was a director of Maguire and Gatchells, the very successful hardware firm on Dawson Street. A business man, he would have been instinctively attuned to supplying people with what they wanted.

Two members were later signalled out at this time for particular commendation for organising the social activities that contributed so much to the club's revival: Denis Hegarty and Cecil Dickson. The events they organised included dances, a club sweep on the Grand National, and – with the additional assistance of Messrs Maunsell, Coall and Reddy – a whist drive. Nothing remarkable there you might say but apparently it all made a significant contribution to club finances. Helpful, too, at this stage was a profit from billiard activities; this was directed to re-furbishing the billiard room which had again fallen into some decrepitude.

Denis Hegarty later had a distinguished career with the Dublin Port and Docks Board, rising to be general manager. In his time with the NYC committee he certainly showed considerable zeal. At the 1937 annual general meeting, he presented a report, recommending, inter alia, converting the reading room into a cocktail bar lounge 'available to both sexes'. A motion supporting Denis Hegarty's proposal was proposed (successfully) by the Hon. Secretary, Sealy Jeffares, the one-time musical comedy performer who was still active in the affairs of the club thirty years after he was first noted in the minutes.

A change crying out for proper attention in these years was the uncertain position of women in the club membership structure. Heretofore, lady guests, as will be remembered, were confined to the boathouse, the coffee room and the roof. Adair Magauran and

Dr. Maunsell, feminists *avant la lettre,* tried unsuccessfully at an EGM on 29 April 1934 to have women admitted as associate members, but failed – by one vote – to get the required two-thirds majority. But the tide was turning.

The following year, the Rear-Commodore, Jim Waller, tried again, and succeeded. But it was a close run thing. His original resolution read:

> That ladies be admitted as Lady Boathouse Associates., the subscription to be one guinea. In the case of a wife or the daughter of a member or a lady residing not less than 15 miles by road from the club, the subscription to be half a guinea (10/6) per annum. That such members be given the full use of the boathouse and its amenities, and the full use of the dining room for the purpose of obtaining refreshment. That such members shall have no voice or authority in the management of the club or the premises thereof. That members shall not play cards in the club unless accompanied by a member in full membership who shall take part in the game, and then only in the dining room. Seconded by P.A. McDermott.

W.B. Stuart tried tacking on an amendment to Waller's proposition by which ladies would be elected annually, without subscription, for the sailing season only, allowing them the use of the boathouse and dining room for refreshment but not allowed to introduce guests. This got nowhere – 20 voted against, 11 for.

Initially, Waller's proposal, when put to the meeting, failed to reach the two-thirds majority (27 for and 17 against). But then, taking his cue from Stuart's amendment, he added the word 'annually' to 'admitted' and this did the trick. The motion was carried, 32 voting in favour of the amended proposal, and 13 against.

Jim Waller's was a significant victory. From then on, there was no barrier – effectively – against women using the club's facilities. Full membership, however, was not conceded until 24 March 1986 when 145 voted for admitting women as full members, 43 against. A well thought-out and reasoned proposal by Barry White,

SC convinced the membership of the need for change. (It was welcomed with limited enthusiasm, this member noted, by some women associates who pointed out that they would now have to pay the full subscription.)

The wonder has to be that, in the 1930s, it took so much effort to overcome the membership's inherent misogyny. After all, women, in the 1930s raced and in some cases owned their own boats. And Dublin Bay Sailing Club, the *de facto* racing arm of the Dún Laoghaire waterfront clubs since its inception in 1884, accepted women members without ever having to have an argument about it.

Women racing in the bay in the 1930s were by no means inconsequential people. Sheila Armstrong raced a Water Wag since 1932. Her father was the solicitor Arthur Armstrong, a member since the days of the Absolute Club, a committee member and also a trustee. Sheila was a ruthlessly competitive sailor. Her favourite ploy, so it was said, was to lure an unwary opponent into committing an infringement, and then cry out triumphantly, in that very distinctive south Dublin voice, 'Go *home*, go *home*'.

Florence Newsom continued to sail the Water Wag she raced with her husband many years after his death. Two women members of Major Waller's own family raced, his wife, Beatrice in the Water Wag of the same name and a Miss Lucy Waller, probably a niece. There was also Dr Margaret Gregg, who lived at the Palace, Shrewsbury Road, and judging by that address was probably the daughter of the Church of Ireland Primate. Another active woman sailor was the Hon. Hester Plunkett, who sailed her own Twenty One Footer, *Maureen*, and who awarded a prize to the Twenty One Footer class for Thursday evening races, thereby giving a fillip to mid-week racing, which in those pre-war years played second fiddle to the Saturday series.

Many National Yacht Club members were active in the racing scene those years in Dublin Bay, both on the water and on the administration side. Adair Magauran, besides sailing his own cruiser, *Eileen,* was for thirty years Hon. Secretary of DBSC and, simultaneously served on the committee of the National Yacht Club for three years. Newsom was for a time a DBSC Hon. Treasurer and besides racing in the Wags with his wife, Florence, also sailed the Twenty Five Footer, *Punctilio,* with J.B. Stephens. He was Vice-Commodore of the National from 1921 to 1931 – effectively Commodore since the actual Commodore position, formally held by the Earl of Pembroke, was a purely honorary one.

Afloat, the most noteworthy change in the 1930s was the recognition that there was need for a new variety of one-design racing craft in Dublin Bay – something more in tune with the bleaker economic times and easier to manage than the Water Wag, less liable to capsize in heavy weather and not quite so ruinous on the pocket as the other one-design boats in the bay like the Twenty-five Footers, the Twenty Ones or the Seventeens. One-design, it had to be; the concept, so it is said, originated in Dublin Bay because the money wasn't available in Ireland to keep up with the constant design changes that handicap racing entailed.

Here the unlikely figure of John B. Kearney enters on the scene. Unlikely, because, unlike most members of the Dún Laoghaire clubs, he was a man who had actually earned his living with his hands. Apprenticed as a shipwright to his father, he joined the Dublin Port and Docks Board in 1900 – as a shipwright – rose in the ranks, and remained there until he retired with the rank of Superintendent of the Engineers' Department. In the Port and Docks he was remembered for some ingenious and remarkable solutions to wharf construction problems.

By the time he came to prominence in the Dublin Bay, Kearney had risen beyond that. Having studied naval architecture in his spare time he became the designer and builder of some remarkably successful sailing craft. Among them was *Mavis,* which in the 1930s raced successfully in the Small Cruisers class. He started racing in Dublin Bay in 1912 and presumably at the same time joined the Edward Yacht Club (as it then was) but was not recorded attending meetings until 1932.

It was at a DBSC committee meeting on 20 March 1933 that he presented the plans which he had prepared at their request of a

John B. Kearney

the new type of boat – that which eventually became known as the Dublin Bay Mermaid. The plans and the establishment of the new class were approved at the subsequent AGM on 10 April, after a discussion described in the *Irish Press* as 'protracted' and in the minutes as 'exhaustive'.

The Commodore, Dr. Wright, explained why the committee decided to consider providing a new class. The formal motion approving the accompanying design was proposed by the DBSC's Hon. Secretary J.A. Magauran (who later that year joined the NYC committee). It reads:

That the plans prepared by Mr. J.B. Kearney and submitted
to the meeting be adopted as a class in the club for a period of
three years from the1st of May and that in the event of three
or more boats of the new class being in commission during
the coming season the Committee shall have power to provide races and prizes.

Among the objectors was a Mr. Snow who thought the new
design would be 'detrimental to the Wag class'. Nevertheless, the
Committee's view prevailed (nemcon) and they had a further motion passed voting the best thanks of the club to Mr. Kearney for his
valuable assistance 'so freely given'.

It was some time before any boats appeared.

The first Mermaid to race in Dublin Bay was Lt. Col. Dwyer's
Amy, which Dwyer managed to enter at the tail-end of the 1935 season. She raced on three occasions in the autumn of that year. She
seems to have done well enough in the Unclassified Boats Class,
which included stalwarts like the *Acushla, Punctilio* and *Nepenthe,* as
well as Lance McMullen's self-built day-boat, *Pelican.* Against such
opposition, *Amy* did well to win the Smalldridge Cup for the Round
Dalkey Island Race.

In due course up to nearly 200 Mermaids were racing nationally.
But that was post-war.

Paradoxically, the bleak economic climate that had favoured the
design of the Mermaid also discouraged it from reaching its true
market potential. Hardly a dozen Mermaids were racing before the
outbreak of the Second World War.

Meanwhile, Kearney being Kearney, he continued to tinker with
the design of the boat, adding such improvements as he judged fit.
This caused some consternation among members of what was supposed to be a one-design class. (It wasn't really, some point out –
more a development class).

Strong words were exchanged. Eventually, Con Manahan, who
later became the Chief Architect of the Board of Works, was asked
to produce what became the official plans of the Dublin Bay Mermaid.

Kearney was unrepentant. 'Sailing is a sport,' he told Con Manahan, 'not war.' (An unexceptional statement, you might say, but some might say that it needs qualification.) The official plans were revised again afterwards by Terence Mallagh. Later, Jonathan O'Rourke, of the National Yacht Club, on behalf of Dublin Bay Sailing Club, became the official custodian of all the Mermaid plans, if anyone wished to inspect them.

Unlike many creative people, Kearney showed no hesitation about getting involved in the chores of administration. He served on the committee of DBSC from 1933 to 1938, interesting himself in such thankless matters as looking after racing marks. One of his useful ideas was to ask his employers, the Dublin Port and Docks Company, to store DBSC marks over a winter, service them and then re-position them before the start of the season. Many of his successors must have envied such useful access to the Ports and Docks facilities.

Unusually – and this is a measure of his standing with the club membership – he was for three years trustee of the National Yacht Club before he joined the Committee. He served as Vice-Commodore from 1942 to 1947.

Kearney's contribution to sailing was immense, both in home waters and elsewhere. Since the boat first sailed in Dublin Bay in the autumn of 1935 there have been Mermaid fleets at Skerries, Malahide, Howth, Clontarf, Wexford, Foynes and, of course in Dublin Bay where in 1964 there were 58 Mermaids entered for racing.

And, then, of course, there was the string of designs for many prize-winning yachts, one of which, *Mavis,* owned and steered by Kearney himself, won many prizes, locally and off-shore.

He was also a key figure in the Irish Cruising Club. And, by virtue of his involvement with both Dublin Bay Sailing Club and the National Yacht Club, he was a party to most of the decisions affecting racing and club management in the bay at the time and which, despite the bleak economic environment, reinvigorated the sailing scene during and after the Emergency years.

11.

The Emergency and Aftermath

Peeople who remember The Emergency are now a dwindling generation. For those not familiar with the term, this handy euphemism is taken in Ireland to refer to the period of the Second World War (and its immediate aftermath) without acknowledging any involvement in it. The term was widely used and generally understood. You even find it in the minutes of the Dublin Bay Sailing Club, the Hon. Secretary Adair Magauran varying it a little by describing it as the *present* emergency.

For survivors, the expression evokes memories of food and fuel shortages, of rationing and ration books, of horse-drawn transportation, of monotonous (but, it now transpires) moderately healthy diets. Children grew up who never tasted bananas, grapes or other fruits. In south County Dublin, as in other urban localities, cherished suburban gardens were torn up so that their owners could, like their forebears, grow potatoes, cabbages and turnips. Misery abounded. People prayed lot, prompted not so much by piety as by the imminence of the death and destruction raining down on English cities a bare sixty miles across the Irish Sea.

Some sailors discovered that ownership of a yacht enabled them to overcome transportation problems in a way not available to others. *The Irish Times*, on 9 July 1943, reported:

> The O'Rahilly and Mr. Sean McBride, barristers-at-law, and
> Mr.J.P. Tyrrell, solicitor, travelled by sea from Dublin to

Wicklow to attend Wicklow Circuit Court on Wednesday. The yacht, which is owned by The O'Rahilly, arrived in time for the opening of the Court. When the Court business was over, the lawyers discarded wig and gown and sailed off on their return cruise to the city. (The yacht in question was the 17 Footer, *Deilginis*).

Through all this, the Dún Laoghaire clubs seem to have managed to get by surprisingly well. But there was, however, a scare in the National during the first summer of the emergency, when it transpired that a considerable body of the membership had held back from paying their subscriptions.

Things at the time looked so serious that at the annual general meeting in June the Commodore, T.J. Hamilton, wondered whether the club could carry on. Members who attended the meeting were extremely annoyed; there were harsh words about the lack of consideration on the part of people who expected the Committee – in very adverse circumstances – to run the club without providing them with the means to do so.

There was indeed something which seems to have niggled members and it needed clarification. If the club went under, would they be liable for its debts? The meeting adjourned to allow the Committee to decide whether they could carry on or else take the fatal decision to shut the place down – and to determine what would be members' liabilities in that eventuality.

To everyone's relief, at the September meeting the Commodore, T.J. Hamilton, was able to announce that the crisis had passed. The alarm bells had had the desired effect, and people were rallying round. As for liabilities in the event of the club shutting down, it emerged that they would be to the extent of their membership subscriptions only. New members would be liable for nothing at all – a useful piece of information, Hamilton pointed out, which would remove any inhibition on members encouraging their friends to join. Hamilton also mentioned an interesting concession – members could be elected for the period 10 January 1940 to 31 March 1941 on payment of a subscription of two guineas.

The Emergency had been real enough. Three years afterwards, at that year's AGM, a long-time member, Arthur Seale, who more than likely had had been through other crises in the past, confessed that in 1940 there had been little hope that the club could survive. That it did – and, moreover, was now in a healthy financial state – he attributed to the untiring efforts of Commodore Hamilton, aided by a very able committee.

That healthy state of the finances continued. At the end of the Emergency, the club had 241 members and no debt. During the 1945 AGM, the Hon. Treasurer, Peter McDermott, could report that income had increased in the last year by £189. Things were even better in 1946 when he could report that revenue had increased by £396 over 1945 and that there was a surplus of £510 of revenue over expenditure.

Strangely, racing in the Bay during the Emergency does not seem to have suffered very much, though, owing to the unavailability of spares, people had to sail their boats much more carefully than ever before. On the last summer before the war, the total of boats entered for racing weekly in Dublin Bay was 89. Over the next four years (1940-1943) it averaged 83. That entries went up to 95 in 1944 and 115 in 1945 is attributable to Snipes and 12 Footers joining the racing – the first signs of the post-war expansion of dinghy racing. Crewing, on the other hand, was obviously a problem. There are references in the various club minutes to members leaving to serve in different armies and navies –all clubs had 'on service' lists which kept memberships alive without the obligation to pay the usual annual subscription.

Later, at the start of the 1952 season, a yachting correspondent in *The Irish Times* offered an interesting explanation as to why sailing did not fall away during the Emergency:

> ... when cars were off the roads, a lot of young men who normally spend their spare time and spare cash on sports cars, motor cycles or continental holidays, found that sailing was the one exciting sport which was relatively unaffected by war shortages. Boats which had been lying neglected on the hard

for years were renovated, launched and raced by a collection of people, who, by their unfamiliarity, brought new life and a new enthusiasm to the sport.

Ireland had no navy of its own, under the 1921 treaty arrangements, until Britain withdrew from the Irish ports in 1938 (Cork, Berehaven and Lough Swilly).The declaration of neutrality imposed an obligation to set up a naval service to patrol and protect the country's territorial waters. Not an easy undertaking in the times that were in it. During World War II the country's total naval strength consisted of no more than six motor torpedo boats, two inshore patrol boats, one mine-layer and one sail-training vessel. Small as it was, there was still a need to supplement the regular naval personnel with volunteers. Hence the Maritime Inscription, drawn from yachtsmen and qualified seamen whose main responsibility was port control and ship examination.

At least fifteen National Yacht Club members enlisted, including Pierce Purcell, then a Dún Laoghaire borough engineer, who succeeded T.K. Hamilton as Commodore in 1944. There are some familiar NYC names among the seven who received commissions at a ceremony in the Port Control Centre on 27 June 1942: Peter Odlum, Sam Smalldridge, A. Thompson, D. Sullivan, Pierse Purcell, Terry Roche, Harry Boyd, M.M. D'Alton and Des Beirne.

From the newspapers of the time it seemed the only activities the men of the Maritime Inscription occupied themselves with were dances and church parades. In Cork, indeed, they made quite a thing of the church parade, with a band in attendance and marches through the main thoroughfares. But port control could sometimes be a stressful and potentially lethal activity. Out beyond the Irish waters there were ongoing deadly conflicts between Allied shipping and German U-boats. Challenging and mounting unknown vessels approaching an Irish port required strong nerves as well as an alert intelligence.

To judge by an article in *Irish Maritime Survey* (1945), as an ancillary to the permanent Marine Service, Maritime Inscription personnel could be involved in an extraordinarily wide range of activities. For instance, they could be engaged on local inshore patrols in harbours and bays, they assisted in the examination service in controlled ports, they could be ordered out to examine strange objects at sea, to assist in mine-laying and mine sweeping, to attend buoys, to assist in the defence of the ports, to manage cables and lights or to undertake salvage and rescue activities. 'Like their parent body, the marine service, they are a fighting service and are trained as such in addition to their ordinary training as seamen', according to the article.

And the origin of the term Maritime Inscription? In its issue of 5 November 1940, the *Irish Examiner* supplied what seemed a possible answer: the old-time navigators used to keep a manuscript containing the names of the men who sailed with them. 'Only qualified seamen could write their names on this document. Hence Ireland has reason to be proud of the name Maritime Inscription.'

However, this is mere surmise and the reality may be somewhat different. Credit for the name must go to Col. Anthony T. Lawlor, OC of the Marine Service and a man of considerable erudition. From his reading, he was aware of to the system for registering seamen set up in the time of Louis XIV by his Finance Minister and Minister for the Marine, Jean Baptiste Colbert. The French service was originally entitled *Systeme des classes* but changed in 1795 during the Revolution to *l'Inscription maritime.*

This was the model used for the Irish service but there were differences. The Irish system was voluntary, whereas the French was intended to enable seamen to enlist in the navy in place of compulsory military service. It had a number of benefit provisions that made it, in theory at any rate, much more humane than the English system of press-ganging seamen. It was abolished in 1965 during national service reforms.

Most, and probably all, of the NYC members who enlisted in the Marine Inscription have gone to their reward but some memories persist. There was an occasion when members of the Dún Laoghaire shore company were ordered go to sea late at night on the tug *Noray* on a mysterious mission. In total darkness, they went ashore at a north Dublin harbour and took control of their target – an establishment run by a certain Joe May. Inside was a crowd of happy bona fide travellers, who on catching sight of armed men in naval uniform assumed they were invaders from a German submarine and panicked. Total mayhem ensued, people diving under tables and so on. This action afterwards passed into local legend and is known as the Invasion of Skerries.

By the summer of 1944, things had returned sufficiently to normality for the members to the National Yacht Club to get worked up about what must have been an outrageous case of bad behaviour. Not that bad behaviour of any kind should ever be regarded as the mark of normality but, as we all sadly know, there has always been a sub-stratum of the National's membership whose aim in life was to try the patience of the most patient of club administrators.

On this occasion 86 members attended a meeting called to endorse or not a decision by the Committee to suspend two members. The record doesn't show why, except that Dan O'Connor made a motion asking:

> … whether the meeting thinks that the conduct of these two gentlemen could properly be held by the Committee to be derogatory or inconsistent with the character of a gentleman or injurious to the interest of the club and whether they merit expulsion.

Mr. W.R. Carson then advised shortening the motion to 'whether these two gentlemen on the 26th. April last were guilty of ungentlemanly conduct'. More haggling ensued, resulting in Dan O'Connor withdrawing his original motion and substituting it with, 'that this meeting do not expel these two members from the club'. This motion was then carried by a large majority, 71 votes to 15.

No bad behaviour, then, and no expulsions. There was still a problem, however – some of the sterner members of the Committee appear not to have been disposed to accept the verdict of the special meeting. At the annual general meeting, which took place just four days later, the Commodore, T.J. Hamilton, declared that he would not accept re-nomination. This was followed by the Rear-

Commodore, J. Spiro, declaring that he, too, was not accepting re-nomination. The Hon. Secretary, R.D. Clark, followed suit, as did the three trustees, Arthur Armstrong, W. J. Nicholl, and K.D.M. Daniel (Ken Daniel was the father-in-law of Hal Bleakley, a one-time DBSC Commodore and for ten years DBSC's principle race officer). J.J. O'Leary refused as well a nomination as Rear-Commodore. The vacancies, of course, were duly filled but an air of unexpressed anger persisted.

Nowadays no one knows what was the particular transgression that so engaged the NYC membership in 1944. Some moral iniquity that could not be spoken about? Or was it simply an old-fashioned row, with blows exchanged and, perhaps (being fanciful) bottles flying in the air? Whatever it was, no one who was present spoke about it afterwards and the whole affair remains a bit of an enigma. Anyway, it all faded away and things resumed their normal course. (J.J. O'Leary, who refused the Rear-Commodore nomination, later became Commodore.)

Sad to relate, the W.R. Carson who tried to amend Dan O'Connor's motion died some two years later in a drowning accident in Dún Laoghaire Harbour. His full name was William Roland Carson and he was a Staff Officer in the office of the Accountant-General in Dublin Castle. Before that, he had worked at the Revenue, specifically on estate duties. In his Trinity days, he had joined the Officers Training Corps which, when the 1914-1918 war broke out, led to a commission in the British army. He suffered from gas poisoning during the war but not seriously enough to interfere with his sailing afterwards. He had qualified as barrister but never practised. He had been elected to the National Yacht Club committee just over two months earlier on 21 June 1946.

It had been Carson's custom, during the summer months, to row out to his yacht, the Kearney-designed *Ain Mara,* and spend the night aboard. In the morning he would have a swim in the harbour before going to work. On Sunday night, 8 September 1946, he entertained some friends at the National's end-of-season dinner and was in his usual good spirits. He rowed out to *Ain Mara* and was not

The J.B. Kearney-designed (and built) 36 foot yawl Ain Mara, *on which W.R. Carson slept during summer months*

heard of until Charlie Gilmore, the Harbour Constable, found his body floating in the harbour. His clothes were located on the boat. For the Harbour Master, Commander Sheil, it must have been painful to have to identify the body; he had been in Carson's company at the dinner in the National the night before.

Dan O'Connor, at the time, could not have been very long a member of the National. His son, also Dan, the Dragon sailor (and now sailing a Water Wag) recalls that when his father acquired a 12 foot dinghy he and Peter McGloughlin used to keep it originally at Bulloch and sail it across to the DBSC starting line in Dún Laoghaire Harbour. This wasn't sensible and they both joined the National from where they sailed the 12 Footer together for many years.

This was the International 12 Foot Dinghy which, by the time it came to be raced under the DBSC burgee, had been around for some time. It was, in fact, a pre-World War I design, produced in 1912 by a gifted amateur, George Cockshott, as an entry for a competition for a yacht tender. It proved a popular design and International 12 Foot, as it came to be known, was raced in a number of European countries, including Britain, France, and Belgium. It was adopted by the International Yacht Union in 1920 and raced in the Olympic Games in 1920 and 1928. It was raced by a number of Irish clubs before the Second World War, including the Seapoint Boat Club, Kilbarrack, Howth and Sutton.

Dublin Bay sailors, in later years, developed their own version of the 12 Footer. Sometime in 1969, when the International 12 Footers were under some pressure from the popularity of both the IDRA 14s and the Enterprises, J.J. O'Leary made some helpful suggestions which provided the class with a much needed boost in Dublin Bay.

These were put into effect by a local class sub-committee (Jack Egan, Alf Delany and Bernard Nolan), probably in consultation with the boat-builder, Edwin (Skee) Gray. The local 12 Footer that emerged from all this was much more suited to Dublin Bay conditions; the mast had been brought back by about two feet, a foredeck installed, and a jib resembling the Wag version added, with the mainsail area reduced from 100 to 80 square feet. Brightly-coloured Terylene sails replaced the cotton variety. These changes had a most beneficial effect with more involvement by the crew, drier boats upwind and downwind and less tendency for the boat to bow-dive when off the wind.

Dan O'Connor and Peter McGloughlin in their modest International 12 Footer were the precursors in Dublin Bay of the dinghy wave which was about to surge over yacht racing everywhere after the Second World War. In 1944 there were five 12 Footers racing from the Dún Laoghaire clubs (besides four Snipes). In 1945 this had grown to seven and the Snipes also to seven. In 1946 came the revolution – or something like it. Out of the blue, *fifteen* IDRA 14s suddenly entered for racing in Dublin Bay, including two by the National's most prominent members, Peter Odlum and J.J. O'Leary. The following year, *eleven* Fireflies joined the dinghy fleet.

It was the same all over Ireland. In twenty-three separate clubs – somebody calculated – young people were discovering the joys of sailing a small boat, which was a totally different experience to sailing the heavier, less responsive craft sailed by their more propertied elders. For some, sailing dinghies was something like a new dimension; it was as though you were conjoined to the elements, through the tips of your fingers on the tiller, and could sense the forces of wind and sea in balance. A new beatitude.

The people involved in the various clubs were talking to each other about coordinating standards for competitions and inter-club racing. There was a lot of communication between clubs. Soon came a realisation that a central organisation to regulate things was needed and out of this came the Irish Dinghy Racing Association. It held its first meeting at the end of March 1946 with a strong Dún Laoghaire representation. Douglas Heard was elected president, Billy Mooney was Hon. Secretary and Peter Odlum joined the Committee.

As you might expect, it took the clubs some time to adjust. In his history of the Howth Yacht Club, Winkie Nixon relates how its Hon. Secretary, Gerald Fitzgibbon, couldn't get his head around the facility with which dinghy sailors hopped between boats and classes. In Dublin Bay safety became an issue like never before. Dan O'Connor found himself on the Dublin Bay committee representing dinghies and emphasising the need for dinghy sailors to wear safety belts and have safety cushions (something like buoyancy bags, seemingly) installed in their boats.

It was 1951 before a rescue launch was provided. This attracted the ire of keelboat owners in that they were paying for a facility they didn't need. They were joined, surprisingly, by Sheila Armstrong and Peter Odlum – Peter because, having rescue experience elsewhere, he was unsure of its efficacy; Sheila probably because she was in the Wag class which observed the rule that if a boat capsized in your vicinity, you stood by to render assistance.

The keelboat ire simmered for years. This used to be countered by the following argument: keelboats gained from subsidising dinghies in that having started in dinghies and having gained valuable sailing experience you then carried it into keelboats. This process was once described by the late Gerry Callanan in characteristically stark terms:

> First you get bitten and you get a dinghy. Then you get wet, then you get piles, and then you get sense and you get a keelboat.

There was also the problem of storing dinghies, which could not be moored like keelboats and moorings were scarce anyway. Most members nowadays do not realise how recent is the club's spacious boat-parking platform. Within recent memory, the sea came up to the club wall. Michael Rothschild, still racing, remembers how during a stag party he and his friends tossed the groom through the dining room window. This was John Mulligan (now sadly departed), a distinguished engineer in his day. There was sufficient water below to allow John to swim around to the Coopers' Slip, as the old lifeboat slip was then called, and in due course regained the company of his rowdy friends.

But it took some years and a lot of money – not always willingly parted with – before the club could provide a proper parking area for dinghies and, coincidentally, keelboats in winter-time.

12.

Of Myth and Legend, 1946-1950

J.J. O'Leary

In the days before club caterers got round to servicing regattas, it was the job of wives and girlfriends to provide hungry sailors with soup and sandwiches after racing. One such wife, serving J.J. O'Leary and the crew of *Fara* after an RIYC regatta, asked him how he had got on.

'Fine enough,' replied J.J., 'until we ran into a fleet of small boats. We went round them, as required, but then that bounder Hollwey, who was behind us, came along and sailed right through them. Do you know him?'

'I should hope so,' said the Colonel's lady, 'I'm married to him.'

Thereupon J.J. made one of those masterly recoveries that put him among the top businessmen of the day. 'Well, in that case,' he said, 'you'll know what's he's like yourself.'

There are many such stories about J.J., who in his day was a figure of myth and legend. Friend of film stars, actors, politicians, journalists, he went everywhere, knew everyone. It was said that a brother of General Franco, or perhaps it was a brother-in-law, sailed with him on *Fara*. Barry Fitzgerald certainly sailed with him for about three years. They were old friends, having known each other as young men when they worked in the Land Commission; they left the civil service on the same day – J.J.to Fleet Street, Barry to the world of the theatre and ultimately Hollywood.

On one occasion they sailed up the Liffey and went ashore, looking for somewhere to eat. Hardly had they sat down at a table in a Cafolla café when they were surrounded by an excited crowd of fans. Barry had been recognised. He handled them all with his customary civility, after which they finished their meal. J.J. was not impressed. He insisted that Barry should pay for the meal since it was all about him meeting his fans.

As a publisher and owner of Cahills, the only largescale letterpress in Dublin where he published in paperback shameless abridgements of novels such as the *Last of the Mohicans*, bus time tables, Dáil reports, *The English Digest, the Irish Digest* and, famously, *The Bell*. It was said that he had a monopoly in the printing of bibles in every African language. He had an awkward relationship with *The Bell's* editor, Sean O'Faolain, a friend of sorts, whom he occasionally brought sailing in *Fara*. In one of his letters, O'Faolain referred to him as 'Jacky O'Leary'. At Cahills, he employed young journalists at the start of their career to do the editing, with O'Faolain as supervising editor at a fee of £1,000 a year.

J.J. was Commodore from 1946 to 1950. During his tenure of office, there were definite signs of recovery after the grim Emergency years, although there was still rationing and scarcities continued. In 1946 it was announced that the Committee:

… had arranged a very complete plan of new club moorings. When laid down these moorings will provide safe holding for approximately 50 boats of all dimensions up to 40 feet overall length and should be a great improvement on the existing arrangements as congestion and risk of damage hitherto existed at this anchorage (*Irish Yachting 1720-1946*, published by the Parkgate Press, which, coincidentally, was J.J.'s publishing firm).

J.J. O'Leary (right) Barry Fitzgerald (centre) and Thekla Beere (left), the first woman to head an Irish government department.

The mooring plan, unfortunately, underestimated the demand and mooring chain was not as easy to provide as first thought. Anchors and chain were in short supply and a there were problems, too, caused by boatmen putting their mooring too close to the National's trot. J.B. Kearney, whose special responsibility this was, dealt briskly with complaints, mentioning, as another example of problems encountered, that the increasing size of the new mailboat was encroaching on the club's mooring space.

The National, like the other clubs, was in fact having difficulty, post-war, in accommodating dinghies, firstly with the International 12 and then 14 Footers. The arrival of the Firefly didn't make things easier. Very much a post-war phenomenon – though, in fact, Uffa Fox's original design dates from 1938 – it had been extensively promoted in the yachting press as a boat for students and young people. The Firefly enjoyed the encouragement of senior members of the Dún Laoghaire yacht clubs; by 1952 Dublin Bay Sailing Club was accepting entries from university sailing clubs without naming members using the boats, hitherto an essential entry requirement.

The Firefly production process at Fairey Marine, the first firm to avail of Uffa Fox's design, favoured block orders from institutions such as university and college clubs. Wood traditionally used in boat-building was in scarce supply but with Fairey Marine this was not a problem. Heretofore involved in war-time aircraft production, Fairey had a surplus of ply and were ideally placed to meet the post-war surge in bulk orders.

The minutes of the 1947 AGM have a cryptic annotation: 'Fireflies. Special facilities for'. Peter Gray, who joined the club in 1950 and whose father, Robert Disney Gray, was Rear-Commodore at the time, thinks that this probably refers to dinghies being moored side to side, with barrels at both ends and a timber plank stretching across to hold them firmly together.

J.J. himself had acquired a Firefly and at one time owned four boats: the Firefly *Siodh Fionn*, plus *Fara*, which was a 'Thirty Square' (an elongated, narrow craft with long overhangs rated by its sail area), the 14 Footer *Dealán* as well as a 52 footer called *Nicolette*.

J.J. was the moving spirit behind the formation of an Irish national yachting authority which, after affiliation to the International Yacht Racing Union, enabled Ireland to compete in the 1948 Olympics. The initial meeting of this body took place on 29 November 1946 in the National Yacht Club with J.J. in the chair. Twenty-two clubs were represented. Other National Yacht Club members present on that occasion were Sean Hooper, Peter Odlum and Terry Roche.

Forming an Irish national body to regulate Irish sailing might today seem uncontroversial but at that time there were difficulties. Some clubs preferred to remain with the body that hitherto performed this function, the British YRA, and there were problems with protest appeals. However, the momentum was for an Irish national body and the inaugural meeting with yacht club representatives from all over Ireland duly took place in the Royal Marine Hotel on Friday, 4 July 1947. The meeting decided to form an authority to be known as the Irish Yachting Federation and to apply for membership of the International Yacht Racing Union. Three National Yacht Club members were elected to the committee: J.J. O'Leary, Sean Hooper and, as its Hon. Secretary, Errol McNally.

The event was marred by an appalling tragedy. Harry Donegan was drowned in Dún Laoghaire Harbour just a few hours after having been elected chairman of the new body. He and four others, his 12-year old son, Jim, his 19-year old nephew Robert Moorhead, and two other solicitors, John Cottrell and John Buckley, were rowing out to Harry Donegan's yacht, *Sybil,* which was moored about 300 yards from the Royal St. George Yacht Club. The intention was to compete in the RSGYC regatta the next day and in the Irish Cruising Club's race to the Clyde on Monday.

It was just after midnight. The sea had become very choppy and about the half way stage, in quick succession, three large waves struck the punt, swamped it and then twice overturned it. All five were thrown in the water. Leaving the other four clinging to the upturned boat, John Cockrell, who was a strong swimmer, struck out for the shore to look for help. On the way, he encountered Joe Lawless, one of the Bulloch boatmen, who had heard the cries for assistance and was on his way.

Despite the atrocious weather Joe, acting with extraordinary courage and coolness, succeeded in getting three of the casualties into his punt – John Buckley, Robert Moorhead and young Jim Donegan. It cannot have been easy, in near total darkness, with a bad sea running which had twice overturned the Donegan punt and the three in the water probably in a state of shock and unable to help themselves. Of Harry Donegan, who could not swim, there was no trace. It was Wednesday before his body was recovered by a local fisherman, James Lambert, picking it in his trawler net fifty yards from the harbour mouth.

Joe Lawless received a lot of praise at the subsequent inquest for his bravery and initiative. Without his efforts, it was pointed out, the tragedy would have been much worse. He worked at the time for J.J. O'Leary on *Fara,* which, on the evening before the regatta, would have accounted for his presence in the area.

Harry Donegan's death was an enormous loss to Irish sailing, particularly on the south coast. He was Vice-Commodore of the Royal Munster Yacht Club, a founding member and Rear-Commodore of the Irish Cruising Club and one of the earliest members of the Royal Ocean Racing Club. His input to the Maritime Inscription in Cork was immense, as would have been his contribution to the new federation, but it wasn't to be. It was J.J. O'Leary and Jimmy Mooney, on behalf of the Federation, who travelled to London in December to negotiate the withdrawal of the Irish clubs from the British body, the YRA.

The British officials, in the event, were not at all unhelpful. They were prepared to facilitate an Irish Olympic entry but didn't see any need to form a separate authority to do so – they could handle it. To the question of whether they would recognise a sub-committee representing Irish clubs, north and south, to deal with matters affecting yachting in Ireland, they replied 'yes probably', adding, inconsequently, that the YRA would be glad if 'the appointed club representatives would attend more frequently at YRA meetings'. What probably resolved the representation issue was word from the IYRU that they would welcome Ireland being separately represented; it would help swell the ranks of the nations participating in the Olympics.

And so Ireland acquired a body to regulate Irish yachting, called the Irish Yachting Federation. After the Olympics at Torquay – at which Alf Delany and Hugh Allen raced a Swallow and A.J. Mooney a Firefly – its functions were subsumed into the Irish Dinghy Racing

Association. Over time this became the Irish Yachting Association, then the Irish Sailing Association and now Irish Sailing.

At the 1948 Olympics, incidentally, Alf had to borrow a Swallow from George O'Brien Kennedy, the boat's co-designer who, fortuitously, lived not far away. It was a local class and there were no such boats in Ireland. An oddity from that event has survived: an invoice to Alf Delany from Messrs Findlater for the food he had to bring with him. Food was still rationed in England at the time and arrangements were made to enable the competitors to bring their own.

By the end of J.J.'s term as Commodore, it became clear that problems relating to the clubhouse could no longer be postponed. During the Emergency and the lean five years that followed nothing other than cursory maintenance was possible. With the passing of the years, improvements – that is the word used – were becoming more and more urgent and at the 1950 annual general meeting there was some wrangling about accessing the subscriptions to carry them out.

There was some murmuring about 'toilets should be taken by pipe from the premises', and John Adair Magauran elicited the costs of the lavatory improvements. There was also a mention of accommodating the small boats (dinghies?) in the boathouse which, apparently, would obviate the need to extend the platform.

A proposal to increase subscriptions was attacked from both ends of the age spectrum; Adair Magauran, not too long a Guinness pensioner, thought it would lead to a loss of older members with fixed incomes, and the youthful Luan Cuffe, then at the start of an eminent architectural career, made a similar plea on the part of the younger generation. An increase of one guinea in the subscription was eventually agreed to, most grudgingly it would seem.

An interesting statistic was quoted during this discussion – there were 104 lady associates. Given that the total male membership came to 341, the female cohort seems surprisingly high. No doubt the Committee must have thought themselves very lucky to have so many lady associates to call on when in late May 1946 they found themselves entertaining officers from a flotilla of ships from the Royal Swedish Navy. These were from the cruiser *Fylgia* and her escorting destroyers *Mjolner* and *Munin*. Their visit to Ireland, according to an *Irish Press* interview with one of the officers, was in recognition of the fact that this country, like Sweden, had been neutral during the recent conflict.

During their Irish visit the Swedish officers were treated most graciously on all sides. The National Yacht Club – and of course its lady associates –entertained them to what seems to have been a splendid dinner and dance. They were also invited to participate in races with boats from the Seventeen Foot, the Twenty One, the Mermaid and the Wag classes. The Swedes won all four races, the locals, no doubt, muttering privately that they were allowed to get away with it 'in the national interest'.

The visit of the Swedish flotilla and the way its officers were looked after made the NYC membership feel good about themselves. At the following general meeting, a Mr. O'Rourke declared that it was a pleasure to be a member of a club which could carry out such successful events. And Jack Martin, speaking in a similar vein, paid tribute to the organisers and singled out the staff for particular mention.

Jack Martin is largely forgotten now, but in his day he was a well-known and highly praised Abbey actor. He was also the grandfather, it turns out, of Paul Maguire, the renowned Dublin Bay Dragon sailor. On Jack's death, Lennox Robinson, an Abbey director and producer at the time, spoke of him thus:

> I remember Jack Martin as one of the most radiant character actors I have ever known in the Abbey Theatre. It was a delight to be his producer and I am sure it was a delight for everyone to act with him, he was so vivid and without self-conceit.

During the First World War, he served with the Dublin Fusiliers and was promoted to captain. Taken prisoner, he managed to produce Abbey Theatre plays like Lady Gregory's *The Rising of the*

Moon and George Fitzmaurice's *The Country Dressmaker* in a prisoner of war camp.

He later retired from the profession and became a bookie, justifying the change on the grounds that as an actor he was having trouble remembering his lines. This seems strange; you would have thought that turf accountancy required an even sharper memory than acting.

Jack Martin had a boat in the Sundries class called *Ben Eadar*, which he sailed with Ned Knight and Charlie Oswald, both founding members of the West Pier Hut team. You might say that on that boat they lived dangerously. In one year, in the autumn of 1947, there were two protests against them, almost in quick succession.

The first was a port and starboard incident involving the 12 Footer *Gillian*, sailed by Colm Cuffe. They were clearly in the wrong, being on port tack, but tried to justify their failure to give way because the proximity of Bulloch mark prevented them doing so. The Protest (Dublin Bay) Committee wasn't having any of it and disqualified them. But then, most unusually, the Committee placed on record their appreciation of 'the manner in which evidence was given on both sides.' Gentlemen all, there were obviously no hard feelings.

Of the second protest, little needs to be said. They were outrageously in the wrong, coming from behind and poking their bowsprit into the boom of F.J. Henry's Water Wag, *Jacqueline*, which was coming through the mouth of Dún Laoghaire Harbour at the time.

13.

Ack Ack Murphy, Sticks O'Herlihy and Friends, 1950-1955

J.J. O'Leary was succeeded as Commodore at the 1950 AGM by A.A. Murphy, known in his time as 'Ack Ack', so-called after the war-time anti-aircraft battery. In those years he was the owner of the Twenty One Footer *Garavogue*. Ack Ack was one of those unfortunates who, however amiable they might be ashore, turned into a veritable Captain Bligh on the water. As one NYC veteran graphically put it, "someone who as soon as he gets a tiller in his hands instantly sprout horns and grows a tail".

Ack Ack did not endear himself to his crew by referring to them as 'they'. This was not wise. 'They' included Michael O'Herlihy, then a noted and very talented theatre designer and later a Hollywood film director. Not an unruly character, exactly, but a man with a mind of his own, and a very unconventional mind at that – a figure of myth and legend very much on a par with his contemporary and friend, J.J. O'Leary.

Among his friends in the National he was known as 'Sticks' O'Herlihy. This is because his surname, by a process of homophonetism, became 'hurley', as in 'hurley stick' and hence 'Sticks' O'Herlihy. Odd, but that's how it's explained by a contemporary.

It is said that on one occasion during a DBSC race, when *Garavogue* was sailing alongside another Dublin Bay Twenty One, Sticks jumped overboard and, with a knife in his mouth, pirate-fashion, mounted the other boat and cut their halyard. It is to be presumed

111

that the rigging of the two boats had become entangled and this was O'Herlihy's way of freeing them.

On another occasion, when he was director and designer of the An Tostal Pageant in Croke Park, he found himself on *Garvogue*, drifting off Bulloch with the time coming dangerously close to the start time in Croke Park. He is said to have jumped overboard, swam ashore and, finding a couple sitting in their car, inoffensively enjoying the view, ordered them to drive him to Clonliffe Road where, still dripping wet in his sailing clothes, to everyone's satisfaction he directed that evening's performance of the Tostal pageant.

And then there was the occasion when Ack Ack had been throwing his weight about, more so than usual, and got on the nerves of O'Herlihy and the other crew members. With *Garavogue* coming up to its moorings, O'Herlihy and company jumped overboard, telling the no doubt apoplectic Ack Ack to go moor it himself. (The clash with Ack Ack was not unparalleled in Dublin Bay. Something similar happened to Jimmy Mooney, who, on the water, if legend is to be believed, also displayed evidence of Captain Bligh proclivities.)

O'Herlihy's transatlantic voyage in *Evora* in the autumn of 1956 is still remembered. There were two others with him on the boat as far as Lisbon, a young Cork engineer, Terry Murray, and Cass Smullen. Cass had to leave them at Lisbon because he had a job to attend to, so O'Herlihy and Murray continued on, first to the Azores, then to the West Indies and on to New York where O'Herlihy had a job waiting for him in television.

Evora was not a large vessel, just thirty feet overall, and not one you would like to take transatlantic voyaging late in the season. It was Kearney-designed, built by Skinners of Baltimore and loaned for the voyage by Dermot Barnes. The plan was to sell it in New York. The departure on 5 September attracted great public interest and there was a huge throng of friends and well-wishers in the National to see them off, including J.J. O'Leary who presented O'Herlihy with a bottle of liqueur brandy 'for medicinal purposes' which didn't last beyond Arklow.

O'Herlihy had a successful career in Hollywood for nearly forty years but never warmed to it or succumbed to its ethos in any way. His wife disliked it intensely and when she lay dying, said to him, 'Take me home. Don't bury me in this horrible place.' Which he did and she was buried in Howth.

He told me this himself during one of our lunches in the National, where I used to meet him after he had retired from film making. He was extraordinary good company, as you might expect. I remember him mentioning he had a vote in the Oscars and I enquired who he voted for. 'Somebody you would never have heard of. A technical person.'

I gathered that actors didn't rate very highly in the O'Herlihy scale of things. He greatly valued people working on the technical side. He had a story of himself and team, out at sea, working on – I believe – an episode of *Hawaii Five-O*. Everyone was very cold and very wet. There was an obnoxious producer present who insisted they continue filming, even though conditions were worsening. Somehow, 'accidentally', a piece of essential equipment got damaged so that everyone was able to go home.

A curious resemblance of something that could happen to overbearing skippers in Dublin Bay, might you think?

It was during A.A. Murphy's tenure of office that the rear of the club began to take on some of the lineaments we're now familiar with. A balcony and the extensive boat parking area was still far in the future, but in 1953 there was pressure from people like Sean Hooper to extend the hitherto rather rudimentary platform on the east side of the clubhouse and to extend the slip. Jim Macken, the Vice-Commodore, one of the partners in the Macken building firm, had this already well in hand: £800 had been set aside for the project which, he said, would not only benefit existing members but encourage others to join.

That, as you might expect, was easier said than done. At the 1954 annual general meeting, Ted Croxon announced that all was now ready, Mervyn Jones had prepared plans, and £1,000 had been set aside but that they were awaiting permission from the Board of

Works. Presumably, this must have been forthcoming for there is no more in the minutes about it.

Ack Ack had some lively people on the committee during his five year term of office (1950-1955). Besides Ted (Edwin) Croxon, who with another National member, Peter Dobbs – both very successful dinghy sailors – set up the Croxon and Dobbs chandlery, it included Alan (Monty) Montgomery, who at this time would have been the Deputy or Assistant Editor of *The Irish Times*. He was later (1961-1963) editor but retired early to take up the more lucrative and less stressful position of publicity director of Arthur Guinness & Co. His boat at the time would have been the 17 footer *Rita*, which he raced successfully for some years with Brendan Ebrill, afterwards Hon. Secretary of Dublin Bay Sailing Club.

As Hon. Treasurer, there was Ireland's first Olympic sailor, Alf Delany who as the owner of the veteran Water Wag, *Pansy*, would have been acutely aware of the needs of the growing dinghy contingent among the NYC membership. His advocacy for dinghies wasn't always successful. Frustrated with the NYC slip which was too steep to allow him comfortably to draw *Pansy* out of the water, he joined the adjoining Royal St. George Yacht Club where the gradient, it appears, was less challenging. But he loyally retained his National Yacht Club membership until his death many years later.

Cyril McCormack, referred to punctiliously nearly everywhere as Cyril, Count McCormack, was another lively member of the NYC committee. In March 1958 he was appointed U.S. director of the IDA but his claim to fame in Dublin Bay would be the spectacular loss on 1 June 1957 of his *Acushla*, one of the last two of the old Dublin Bay Twenty Fives (the other was *Punctilio*). It happened in Balscadden Bay, at the foot of Howth Head. After it had struck a rock and failed to move, Jim Doyle, one of the crew, jumped overboard and established that not only had *Acushla* struck a rock but her keel was jammed firmly between two of them. Successive towing attempts by other boats failed to dislodge her.

And so, when the tide receded, *Acusla's* keel, having nothing to support the weight of the boat, snapped. After that, the boat was irrecoverable despite the large crowd from the cliffs and the other boats that stood by offering to help. There was a lot of negative coverage afterwards, not least because the intrepid Jim Doyle was a Dublin correspondent of the *Cork Examiner*, who no doubt had the unusual experience of writing up a story of which he was a chief protagonist.

Ack Ack's Vice-Commodore at this time was Jim Macken. At this time, he was sailing the 17 footer *Eileen*. A very successful builder, and despite the demands of the day job and his NYC responsibilities, he somehow found time to build his own Dragon, *Aileen*. It was said that the materials came from leftovers from one of Jim's building sites and that the sliding door on the foredeck hatchway was the remains of confession box from a church he had been building. He and his brother-in-law, Brendan Ebrill, raced *Aileen* very successfully, but on the water argued incessantly, so much so that their families refused to sail with them.

Brendan Ebrill

Yet ashore, both were among the kindliest, most genial people you could meet. Jim obviously enjoyed the regard of other NYC officers. When J.B. Kearney died in 1967, Jim discovered Kearney had nominated him executor of his estate.

Ack Ack's Rear-Commodore for most of his term of office was Fred Brownlee who sailed and raced the weird and wonderful *Flying Fox*, designed for him by Uffa Fox. It was 48 feet overall and 36 feet on the waterline. It weighed seven and a half tons, light for a boat of thsoe dimensions. She was, in fact, designed to plane and Fox himself admitted that in light airs or in going to windward in a

The Uffa Fox-designed **The Flying Fox**

heavy sea she could be beaten by heavier boats. With wind off the beam and conditions right she would be able to plane at twenty knots. Fox calculated that it would appeal to sailors who had experience of racing in planing centre-board boats. Fred was among that cohort – he had considerable experience racing in dinghies.

Fred sailed *Flying Fox* locally in DBSC races for three years (1952, 1953, and 1954), with what success the records don't show. However, shortly after he acquired her, in July 1952, competing in the Irish Cruising Club' race to the Clyde, he picked up her moorings at Hunter's Quay *seven* hours ahead of the second boat, Col. J.B. Hollwey's *Viking O*. Conditions obviously were right. Eventually, Fred tired of her uncongenial ways and put a mizzen mast on her so that she went to windward like any other boat of her size. This didn't

The Saddle on **The Flying Fox**

affect her steering in any way: Fred claimed he could sometimes let her steer herself without his having to touch the wheel.

The boat's unique feature was a saddle and stirrups, installed behind the wheel and intended to make life comfortable for the helmsman on long journeys. It didn't impress the editor of *Yachting World* in April 1950:

> Very few horses that we have met have their legs shorter on one side that he other and so canter or gallop   at an angle of heel about 30deg …But perhaps the saddle is intended only for use when she is planing at great speed on an even keel.

The saddle wasn't one of Fox's notorious leg-pulls. It was a real enough. (see photograph). Fred sold *Flying Fox* in 1957, having grown tired, after thirty years sailing in the Irish Sea with what he described as 'short, mostly cold, seasons and a few ports of interest'. This is what he told her new owner, a Mr. A.W. Norrish. Besides, he had bought a new unfinished house and was so enthusiastic planning and decorating it that his interest in sailing had waned. His very successful business also no doubt required his attention, employing more than sixty men assembling Pilot radios at his factory in Molesworth Street.

Ack Ack was a popular and effective Commodore. The spat with O'Herlihy and Co. was just one of those things that happen on the water. At a dinner in his honour when he retired, J.J. who was taking over the Commodore's flag for the second time, spoke warmly of Ack Ack's personality and experience. The club had made much progress during his term in his opinion.

By profession Ack Ack – or to be correct – Alfred Augustine Murphy, was an architect of some standing. In his younger days he won a number of architectural prizes, including the RIAI prize (along with P.J.F. Munden) for a design of a public memorial, the Institute's prize for a fire station and the President's prize for water colour sketches.

After he had retired from the Commodore position in 1955, his doctor ordered him to stop sailing and he had to give up *Garavogue*. The doctor's advice was well taken and Ack Ack lived on for many years later. He died in his eighties on 16 January 1968.

14.

New Horizons, 1956-1960

The middle 1950s marks the beginning of the halcyon days of dinghy racing in Dublin Bay. In May 1955, the first 505 to race in Dublin Bay made its appearance in the National Yacht Club. It was built for two prominent National members, Sean Hooper and Phil Kane. The glamour boat of the period, it was raced by all the top dinghy sailors of the day, including the great Paul Elvstrøm, whom Irish sailors first met at the 1948 Olympics.

The *Irish Field* described it enthusiastically:

> The 505s are Europe's most advanced racing dinghies, mould-
> ed from the lightest veneer (the hull is only 6mm in thickness
> and even her tiller is a hollow box spar) and built rather like
> the wing of a glider. The 505 has flared top-sides and is capa-
> ble of sailing rings around any other dinghy yet produced.

Its only drawback was its price – £300 – which was regarded as bit steep by dinghy sailors of the time.

Sean Hooper's son, Johnny, sailing a 505 with clubmate Peter Gray, son of Robert Disney Gray, became very active in inter-cub racing and built up a formidable reputation at home and abroad. In the 505 Worlds, held in Cork in 1959, they had an easy win in one race though the series was eventually won by a Parisian competitor. On another occasion, at La Boule in Brittany in August 1958, they raced in a winds of 30-40 knots during which their boat capsized and sank (reports differ; another account says they capsized twice and broke a mast).The must have put it all back together pretty smartly because they raced next day and came fifth. This partnership continued, peaking with a first in one of the seven races of the sailing Olympics in the Gulf of Naples in 1960.

This was a pivotal moment for Irish sailing, when two young men from the National Yacht Club, not backed by the resources of countries with longer yachting traditions, were able to prove, if only for one shining moment, that with natural flair and dedication they could take their place among the best sailors in the world.

It was still a totally amateur sport at the time, competitors not being supported by teams of trainers and sports psychologists as is customary nowadays. Peter was not long married to Susan Millar and had a newborn baby, and besides, he had his career in the bank to keep in mind. Johnny had yet to marry Bernie Duffy but he had to devote a lot of time to building up his legal practice. The received wisdom was that to compete in the Olympics you had to 'practice, practice, practice', and this they did relentlessly. They also entered into a tough, keep fit regime, which included running around places in town like the Iveagh Gardens or, locally, along Killiney beach.

The fact that the Flying Dutchman, the class they were to compete in, was not sailed in Ireland was not a great problem. Johnny sourced one in Holland, brought it home, and built an ingenious frame to support it on his Volkswagen without damaging the roof. They called it *Three Leaves*. With this they set out on their great adventure, competing in three European regattas, two in Holland and one in Germany, before reaching Naples.

Peter recalls that racing an unfamiliar dinghy didn't bother them in the least. 'It was just another boat.' What was problematical was shifting winds in the race area in the Gulf of Naples and some haphazard race management. Happily, on 1 September, they won the fourth of the seven races in the series, though not without some argument. The Italian competitor, Capio, actually beat them to the line by thirteen seconds but was disqualified by the Protest Committee for not having rounded the leeward mark. The infringement had been clearly witnessed by an official observer, Peter Scott, the famous naturalist.

The IDRA 14 at this period retained its popularity which it still has to this very day. Some of its principle promoters (Douglas Heard, the Doctors Mooney, *pere et fils*, and Hugh Allen), had met its designer, George O'Brien Kennedy, for a convivial lunch in the old Jurys hotel, one day towards the end of the war. Their requirements had been very specific: it should be dual-purpose rather than an out and out racing design, sea-worthy, sturdy and, above all, moderate in cost, attractive in appearance and modern in design.

O'Brien Kennedy's design matched these specifications to perfection. Obviously, it was never going to appeal to the hot shots or feature in the Olympics, but its sea-kindly qualities appealed to the growing body of dinghy sailors, particularly in Dublin Bay where weather conditions can be sometimes pretty brisk. Its low price was another attraction.

Apart from the IDRA 14s, there were at least two other O'Brien Kennedy-designed boats that sailed from the National, both of the Kerry class. One was a tough, rugged, seaworthy 27 foot cruiser, the winning design in a competition sponsored by *Irish Yachting* and *Motor Boating*. It was suitable for construction by Irish boatyards and aimed principally at the export market. It was successful enough, twenty-six boats being sold. Its principle competitor at the time was the Shipman 28, which catered for the same market and was backed by superior Scandinavian resources.

The Kerry's prototype was *Margaret*, which was bought and sailed in DBSC races by the late Gerry Callinan. The other was *Ring of Kerry* which was bought and cruised extensively by Cormac McHenry. (See also Chapter 16, The Modern Era.)

How Sean Hooper, who was one of the leading members of the Irish Bar, found time to sail a boat is something of a mystery. Reading the newspapers of the time you find Sean Hooper's name occurring time and again, sometimes in quite run of the mill situations, but then occasionally as counsel for the defence in some of the country's most high profile cases.

The *Rose Tattoo* prosecution was one, when Church and State combined to prosecute Alan Simpson and his wife for putting on what seemed even then to have been a harmless Tennessee Williams play. Hooper acted for the defence. (Was it he, by the way, who ensured that some of the press referred to the defendant as 'Captain Simpson', thus ensuring that the defendant was presented as a perfectly respectable person?). There was also the Shanahan Stamps case, when Hooper was defence counsel for the spooky Dr. Paul Singer. And, painfully closer to home, there was the Preston Ball murder case when Hooper defended the son of fellow NYC member (of which more presently).

J.J. O'Leary was into his second term as Commodore in those years, which were marked by some of the membership's recurrent upsurges of concern about the clubhouse upkeep. Not that the premises were allowed to fall into disrepair during Ack Ack's term – somebody had calculated that in an average year about £1,000 was being spent on repairs and renewals – but there was never enough provision left over for the modifications and adaptations needed to bring the premises more into line with changing tastes and expectations. (There is, however, a reference at the 1955 AGM of heavy expenditure on a new platform and slipway in 1954).

Frank Lemass, who had joined the committee in 1957 and formed part of the sub-committee looking at premises requirements, presented a report to an extraordinary general meeting on 18 February 1958. What was being proposed was perfectly within the remit of the committee, but as they themselves were not unanimously in favour of the scheme they thought it well advised to find out what the members thought.

Not much, apparently. At this remove, the proposals don't appear to have been excessively radical: re-decoration of the dining room, the installation of wall lights, and the removal of a partition at the west end of the dining room. There was also a reference to a need for a proper partition with swing doors for service between the dining room and the servery. But the removal of the partition at the west end of the room seems to have involved the elimination of a 'small room' for cards which rankled with some members.

The Hon. Treasurer, J.R. Clark, was decidedly among those against. He detailed numerous urgent items of necessary expenditure and pointed out that 'the present time was a bad time to embark on further expenditure of a non-essential nature'.

Of the same opinion, was another committee member, Herbert 'Flick' Hardy, a well-known Mermaid sailor and manager of Tyler Shoe Shops, and who, as retailer, would have had direct, personal experience of the 'bad time' that was in it.

J.R. Clark returned to this theme at the subsequent AGM on 21 March 1958:

> ... there has been growing anxiety about the state of trade in the near future. Nearly everyone believes that it will be one of strain which may be severe...in view of this outlook, I sincerely hope that the members will not expect the committee to work miracles or to embark on any expensive schemes which may ultimately lead to a demand for an increased subscription.

Indeed, no one did at that meeting but the proponents of a rejuvenated clubhouse had not gone away. At the 1959 annual general meeting, Willie Maguire, later Commodore, an architect by profession and a man of considerable persuasive powers, succeeded in having a sub-committee set up which would report on *all* existing club facilities and accommodation, and 'make recommendations by which the present amenities may be improved'. There was also an obligation on the sub-committee 'to investigate ways and means by which their recommendations may be implemented and financed'.

This they duly did the following November, and presented their report with such professional élan that the customary objectors could make no headway. Miraculously, the whole package was accepted, including that the scheme was going to cost the hitherto unimaginable sum of £10,000. A finance sub-committee was set up to handle the finances, including some members who would have wider financial perspectives than most, such as Liam Boyd, head of Trans World Airlines in Ireland, and Cyril Widmer, of Wates Homes. What's more – and with all due respect, no doubt, to J.R. Clarke – the meeting increased the annual subscription from eight guineas to ten.

It certainly reflects very well on the membership of the National Yacht Club that in such a discouraging economic climate (emigration in those years was averaging 43,000 a year) they were able to look beyond their immediate difficulties and confidentially undertake an ambitious and fairly costly refurbishment project.

There were one or two bright spots to lighten up the encircling gloom. At the 1952 annual general meeting, Clement Griffin, supported by Dan O'Connor, succeeded in persuading the members to set up a separate cadet membership category for young people. The age limits were 18 to 25. Gender was not mentioned but since one of the clauses referred to '*his* membership' it can be safely assumed that the possibility of young women wanting to join was not contemplated.

A clause inserted in the rules indicated how cadets could be expelled for misbehaviour but, as it turned out, the members' misgivings were misplaced; a short few years later, the new young members actually brought some glory to the club. J.R. Clark, at the 1958 AGM, digressing from finances, observed:

> ... it is a very heartening thing to see our younger members headed by Mick Geoghegan and Victor Branagan making such an excellent job of the Team Racing as they did. I have no doubt that it added greatly to the credit of the Club.

There would be many more such victories, as the medal display on the mantelpiece in the club dining room can testify.

The Dún Laoghaire sailing community, at this time, were waking up to the need to consider the needs of young people and, incidentally, provide the continuity that would ensure a future for the clubs. It was in this same year of 1958 that Dublin Bay Sailing Club decided to set up its junior section which came into being in January 1959. It thrived for some years, but having lost the lease for its facilities at the back of its West Pier, it fell away when the replacement site in the Coal Harbour failed to satisfy. By this time there was a growing acceptance that young people would have to be separately provided for and that junior sailing become a regular and important part of the club programme (see, under 'Miscellanea',

Carmel Winkelmann's recollections of how the NYC Junior Section came about).

Another advance in 1958 was to purchase an outboard for the club punt to speed up ferrying members to their boats, an innovation which made life much easier for the boatman, Billy Walsh, who hitherto had to row members out to their boats.

Rarely mentioned in club minutes of the period are the social activities that have always been a feature of club life. Dinner-dances, in vogue at the time, (admission price, 4/6) got one mention and there is also a reference to a class dinner. Everyone seems to have an opinion on the catering, often unfavourable – Sean Hooper remarked at one AGM that he would often do better elsewhere. Cuisine seems to have improved towards the end of the decade; closing the 1958 AGM, J.J. remarked with some surprise that no one had thought fit to raise catering as an issue.

The bar, it can safely be assumed, contributed much to brighten the lives of members in that depressed era. Receipts always attracted the attention of members at annual general meetings. The Hon. Treasurer, J.R. Clark, at the 1955 AGM reported that up to 1952 bar receipts had increased steadily, but had dropped in 1953 (no explanation offered) but that in 1954 they had exceeded those of 1952. At the 1956 there is an enigmatic reference by E.J. Cotter to the club having been 'unhorsed' by staff changes and mentioning the need to have an auditor engaged to conduct checks on stocks in the bar, cellar and dining room.

Finally, at the 1959 AGM, discussions on bar finances were shut off altogether when, to the annoyance of some members, separate figures for bar receipts were not disclosed in the annual accounts. J.J. O'Leary, in the chair, had a tantalising response to all this: there was 'necessity for some privacy in presenting the accounts and added that the circularised accounts should not divulge unnecessary details regarding the volume of turnover in the bar'. Commercial sensitivity or was it another motivation altogether? One possibility comes to mind.

Older members will remember that these were the glory days (if that word would be the approved adjective nowadays) of 'bona fide travellers', when large swathes of the city's drinking population de-camped in their motor cars at pub closing time to establishments like Matt Smith's of Stepaside or Eugene O'Reilly's of Santry where they could obtain refreshment on the grounds that they were bona fide travellers (that is, three miles from home). There was a grow-ing outcry at the number of serious accidents resulting from all this traffic and the obloquy was extending to private clubs, the so-called 'drinking dens'.

Was J.J., with keener political antennae than most, anxious to ensure that the National Yacht Club could not be described as a drinking den, where people sat up to the small hours drinking their heads off ? An unworthy thought, surely?

15.

Crisis in the Sixties –
The Car Ferry Controversy

The temporary ferry terminus at East Pier

Of that most numerate of men, Frank Lemass, the club's Commodore between 1960 and 1965, it was once said that even his dog could count.

The assertion was made one Thursday evening by someone in the group he used to meet at the far end of the NYC bar after racing. Frank arrived late on that occasion, accompanied by the alleged number cruncher of a dog, a gentle, well-behaved King Charles spaniel. After he had settled down with his usual Green Spot, the question was put to him: 'Could that dog count?'

'Of course,' said Frank, 'Jack,' he said, turning to Jack Kennedy, 'do a count-down'. Jack was the DBSC timer and indeed Race

Frank Lemass

Officer at the DBSC starter's hut on the West Pier for over forty years. So he obliged, going into the familiar sequence, 'ten, nine, eight, seven, and six . . .'

The dog heard this and clearly was not happy. He sat up, showing clear signs of distress. And then, just when Jack came to the end of the sequence, '. . . three, two, one – gun' the dog shot away, terror-stricken, jumping over tables, scattering the pints and disappearing out the door, thus providing indisputable proof that Frank Lemass had a dog who could count.

There was an explanation, of course. Frank, in those years under doctor's orders not to race, used to take the dog for a walk on the West Pier. When he would come to the Starter's Hut, he would go inside to watch the starts. The dog got used to the starting sequence, but never to the gun. It terrified him, so much so that hearing it he would shoot away as fast as he could. Frank knew very well how it would react to the re-enactment in the NYC bar.

Jack Kennedy, in those years, was presiding figure in the West Pier race management operation. It was said that if you disputed any of his decisions as race officer he was liable not to recognise your boat on the finishing line. That, to be sure, has to be a vile slander because (it could be argued) Jack's eyesight was never too good.

He was much loved in Dublin Bay, except for the odd malcontent. His day job was a sports reporter in the *Irish Press,* to which he regularly supplied DBSC racing results. On the last day of the season's racing, he would sometimes be invited to join the crew of the Lemass boat and, as the boat approached the finishing line, would be given the helm. It was usually a winning boat in those years, which enabled Jack to report to *Irish Press* readers, quite truthfully that 'Frank Lemass's boat, *Fenestra*, with Jack Kennedy at the helm, was the first boat to cross the finishing line in the Saturday's race'.

One last personal memory of Jack Kennedy is of him, in advanced old age, coming out of the National and stopping to look at the crane lifting a substantial cruiser out of the water onto the NYC platform. The NYC head boatman, Jack Brennan, was still on the deck, arms outstretched, holding apart the straps of the slings so that they wouldn't foul the rigging. Jack Brennan, too, was advanced in years. 'Isn't he a great man for his age,' Jack Kennedy was asked. 'Why wouldn't he be,' was the response, 'doesn't he neither smoke nor drink nor have sex – and I have all three.'

Frank Lemass was already well acquainted with the National Yacht Club's varied financial and club-house problems when he became Commodore in March 1960. Yet neither he nor anyone else in that relatively tranquil time of the club's

Jack Kennedy

Jack Brennan

history could have predicted the controversy and political maelstrom that engulfed the Dún Laoghaire waterfront just two years later and for a period threatened the club's existence – or at least its existence on the site it had occupied for nearly a century. The threat at the time was very real and at first seemed difficult to combat: a government proposal to construct a car ferry terminal in the space between the East and Carlisle Pier – effectively land-locking the club and cutting off its members' access to the harbour.

Arguments from Bord Failte and tourist interests for a ferry service between Dún Laoghaire and Holyhead were persuasive: the number of visitors' cars shipped direct from Britain to Ireland in the first ten months of the year was well over 17,000, a 15 per cent increase on the previous year. With the new car ferry facilities, the figure could easily reach 40,000. In the pre-Celtic Tiger era, when employment opportunities were few, these figures mattered.

But who would operate the service and who would provide the ferries? This was occupying the minds of the relevant individuals in the Department of Transport and Power and Bord Failte. The only company with the resources to run cross-channel ferry services at the time was British Railways; it was their officials, apparently, who had pointed out that the East Pier site was the one most suited to a car ferry terminal. The difficulties in putting a terminal in that particular place were not explored in detail at the early stage – perhaps with a view to bringing the British on board.

The National committee, naturally enough, were alerted quite early of what was afoot. At the 1962 annual general meeting on 30 March Frank Lemass had told the members: 'If the National Yacht Club felt obliged to make a change, the Board of Works were co-operative as to providing alternative premises.'

At that stage, and indeed over the next year, the obligation to re-locate was being taken quite seriously by the National committee. Indeed, the *Irish Press*, on 18 July 1963, reported that the club had instructed an architect to design new premises.

> Mr. Frank Lemass, Commodore of the club, said he had no idea where the club would be sited. The Board of Works were very sympathetic and it was hoped they would accept the club's plans when drawn up.

Lemass was perhaps being disingenuous about the prospective new location. Members who were there at the time clearly remember the spot intended: it was where MGM Boats now have their boatyard. Not a particularly prepossessing area for a yacht club, but who knows what could have been made of it, given adequate funding, a progressive committee and a suitable architect?

The *Irish Examiner's* report, on the same date, carried an optimistic gloss on the possible enforced migration:

> Mr. Frank Lemass, general manager of C.I.E., and Commodore of the National Yacht Club, is confident that out of all the upset will come a club-house worthy of the Club – indeed, perhaps, the most modern and comfortable yacht club in these islands. He says that they have instructed an architect to draw up sketch plans for a new club premises and when these were prepared they would have discussions with the Board of Works and tell them what type of club-house they required.

But on the other side of the Channel, some respite was at hand. In his 1962 report to the Annual General Meeting there was a suggestion from Frank Lemass that the project was meeting resistance on the British side. The sentence reads:

> At British Transport Commission level the project has stopped. The Commodore thought it unlikely that the club should be interfered with within this year – or next.

In Britain at this time, a total overhaul of the railway system was in progress, involving the closure of one-third of the network, abolition of the British Transport Commission and its replacement by a new Railways Board. Dr. Beeching, who was overseeing the re-organisation, was reported to be totally opposed to the Holyhead-Dún Laoghaire project; with a new terminal at Holyhead and the inclusion of a new ferry vessel it was likely to cost £3 million. For the head of a company which in 1960 had reported a loss of £62 million in 1960, this was a not unreasonable attitude to a project very peripheral to his main concerns.

Meanwhile, opposition locally to the project was growing without any need, it would seem, for the National Yacht Club's members to go stirring it up. With hindsight, the Ferry's promoters appear to have singularly underestimated the opposition it was likely to meet locally. Jack Corr of the Dún Laoghaire Borough Travel Association made its opposition very clear, spelling out the deleterious effects it would have on the East Pier:

> This would bring about the elimination not only of the National Yacht Club but also of the sun terraces which were the particular attraction of that part of the borough, and which were used every year by thousands of visitors and residents. It would also restrict access to the farther reaches of the Pier itself.

On traffic, he pointed out that while the car ferry service was 'heartily welcomed', that part of the harbour frontage

> ... had the least accessibility for motor vehicles, and which possessed no immediate wide outlets in any direction. On the contrary, the relatively narrow Marine Parade is already congested by moving traffic during the season and the Association views with great apprehension the traffic problem which will be created by the continuous arrival and departure of some 300 vehicles during the busiest period. That the introduction of a new tourist amenity, in the form of a car ferry, should be accompanied by the destruction of existing amenities is contrary to both common sense and public policy.

Dún Laoghaire Corporation were also getting involved, clearly irked at not being consulted. The *Irish Press* reported at the time:

> One of the extraordinary features of the plan was that Dún Laoghaire Corporation had not been brought into consultation at all – but the Corporation has been busy and now the Minister concerned, Mr Childers, is to meet some of its members on next Friday.

The most effective contribution to the controversy was probably Frank Lemass's own interview with John Skehan on RTÉ's *Broad-*

sheet on 12 August 1963 (and still available on *You Tube*). A quintessentially Lemass performance – low-key, good-humoured, not at all argumentative. He acknowledged the necessity for a car ferry terminal at Dún Laoghaire. Members 'can't be resentful of the fact that our need to depart is because of the advent of the car ferry – a good thing.' Yes, he understood the argument why the ferry should not go up-river – 'maybe the disadvantage there is the turnaround time (and) because it is quicker, shorter to come into Dún Laoghaire'.

Then, tentatively, off the cuff, as though it was just a personal suggestion, he broached the possibility of another site: '

> I feel myself that there might be other possibilities in the harbour (which is) quite enormous – a place which should be looked at closely – St. Michael's Wharf – a vast area (behind the Carlisle Pier) – not used at all – completely unproductive – which would be adequate for the assembly of cars – lots of water there. True, not as protected as the other location – but, as this is a summer service you don't get bad gales and bad seas in the summertime.

The St. Michael's Wharf alternative seemed to have been gaining traction later that year when the car ferry project was discussed at a meeting in November in the Queens Hotel of the Dalkey Literary and Historical Debating Society. One of the guest speakers, Mr. K. O'Doherty, a Bord Failte manager, indicated that the Bord was pushing the idea:

> For some time it seemed that the Dún Laoghaire East Pier was the only one possible, but Bord Failte proposed St. Michael's Wharf as an alternative and found the Corporation in agreement. If it were used it would leave existing amenities intact…The final decision rested with the Government – Bord Failte was aware that the Minister for Transport and Power was taking a great interest in the problem and it was hoped that he would be able to announce a decision shortly.

There was an interesting contribution at this meeting from Frank Lemass on a matter which may have already have been giving the Department officials concerned some pause: 'It was clear that the cost of replacing the Club in size and facility would be about £150,000.' They would expect to get that sum from the Government, he said, and he thought they could justify getting it for the enforced move. A not inconsiderable sum at the time.

Meanwhile, British Railways, following discussions between Bord Failte and the British Transport Commission, had finally decided to provide the necessary vessel. This was confirmed by the Manager of that body's London Midland Region, H.C. Johnson, on 9 July 1963, indicating at the same time that a new vessel for the service would be built and was expected to be available by early 1965. The announcement effectively gave the green light to proceed with a terminal, even though Minister Erskine Childers and his officials had yet to decide where exactly that terminal might be sited.

The statement did, however, concentrate official minds to think about a provisional solution: a temporary terminal at the East Pier which would not affect the National's clubhouse or its approaches from the water. It involved a *temporary* (sic) widening of part of the lower deck of the pier to provide four car lanes. On disembarking from the ferry, cars would move down the pier in single file, turn around at the bandstand, and then divide into three lanes until they reach a temporary customs hall which, in theory at any rate, could simultaneously process six cars. They would exit in single lane and from there proceed to Marine Parade.

Though the construction of a temporary terminal at that location would have given some sense of relief to National Yacht Club members, there were others who felt strongly about any interference with the pier, among them Jimmy Mooney, who wrote two very angry letters to the press about out 'ruining the magnificent East Pier of which we in Dún Laoghaire are so proud'. This prompted replies on behalf of the Minister and from the local Fianna Fáil TD, Lionel Booth, justifying the temporary terminal on the grounds that the deadline of July 1965 had to be met, when the British ferry vessel would have become available. If it wasn't met, the British would be justified in moving it to another route. And another four or five years would elapse before another vessel could be provided.

Jimmy Mooney's letters were published in early April in 1964, when work on the temporary terminal had just begun. He had set up a protest body called STEP (Save the East Pier), which the Dún Laoghaire Corporation, at its meeting on 4 May, agreed to meet. Interestingly, at that same meeting, the Corporation had a letter before it from the Minister for Transport and Power 'intimating that he had decided that a permanent terminal should be located at St. Michael's Wharf'.

In truth, it wasn't a great surprise because it was clear for some time that official opinion was moving in that direction. A relief to the members of the National Yacht Club, certainly, that they were not having to move their clubhouse elsewhere but there was a drawback. They were losing a large trot of moorings to make way for the pier extension, which was already under way, according to an *Irish Press* report on 14 February 1964:

> Work has commenced on the new ferry installation at Dún Laoghaire Harbour, and a Board of Works dredger is clearing the area between the mail-boat pier and the East Pier, of all yacht and small boat moorings. A huge steel cable in the harbour bottom to which all the craft moorings are attached, will have to be raised. More than fifty moorings are attached, including those of the National Yacht Club.

This was a source of considerable grievance since the replacement moorings provided at the East Bight ('Up the HAArber', in the boatmen's jargon) were neither as safe nor as accessible as the moorings they were losing. A number of boats were lost there in later years, when mooring warps failed during easterly gales.

Protests notwithstanding, construction of the temporary terminal went ahead and everything was in place when the *Holyhead Ferry 1* went into service in May 1965. Someone has calculated that 69,000 cars passed through the East Pier terminus between then and 14 April 1969 when the terminus at St. Michael's Wharf was opened. It was not very pleasant for the NYC members to have that volume of traffic passing their doorstep, but they did have the compensation that the catastrophe that had earlier seemed a real possibility had been everted.

Frank Lemass relinquished his Commodore's flag at the 1965 annual general meeting. John McConnell, head of the McConnell advertising agency, who took his place paid tribute on that occasion to Lemass's negotiating qualities: 'He had never served under a better chairman, who, in a quiet manner, always got his way.' That quietude of manner was not a quality particularly remarked on when Lemass took the helm of the various boats he sailed over the years with Aidan Brindley – first the Mermaid, *Thumbalina*, then the Dragon, *Aletta*, later, the Twenty Four Footer, *Fenestra* and, finally, in his last years, a cruiser called *Fág a' Bealach*. (The latter title caused Lemass, of a republican family, some unease; it was believed to be the war-cry of the Inniskilling Fusiliers).

He and Aidan Brindley were a very formidable partnership, winning many prizes over the years. When circumstances required, guile was not eschewed. During one port and starboard incident, when the Lemass boat had no rights whatever, Lemass was reputed to have called out angrily, in a voice of thunder, 'port'; this caused the opposing boat to fall back in confusion, before realising they were the victims of an outrageous but perfectly legal ploy.

The partnership was known in Dublin Bay as the Brinner and the Brain. The Brain, obviously, referred to Lemass's cerebral qualities, while the Brinner – well, the Brinner was just Aidan, a man of no known intellectual interests nor at all respectful of convention. (There was a celebrated encounter between the Brinner and Mrs. Doyle, the formidable bar manageress of the Royal St. Yacht Club – a matter of a tie not worn and the exchange of discourtesies that flowed therefrom.) The Brinner and the Brain seemed an incongruous partnership but it lasted over twenty years until Lemass's untimely death, at the age of 63, in 1974.

Frank Lemass's wife was the former Máire McDonagh, a niece of the poet and the 1916 leader. Known as Moll Lemass, she had been a great beauty in her day and there was a very a fine drawing of her by Sean O'Sullivan, RHA, in the Lemass sitting room. She, like Aidan, was no respecter of convention, and loved stirring things up just for the fun of it, it would seem.

At NYC receptions, she was sometimes heard to say, 'when I was a girl, I slept with Michael Collins'. This would have the effect of bringing every conversation within twenty feet to a dead stop before Moll would add sweetly, 'I was two years old at the time'. The explanation was that McDonagh's was a safe house during the Troubles and Collins did,

Moll Lemass

indeed, occasionally sleep there in whatever bed was offered, even if it meant sharing it with a sleeping child.

She made much of her McDonagh family connection – poets, writers and literary folk ('unlike the Lemasses, who were just business people'.) This could take an odd turn at times. Moll got involved in a charity that looked after travellers, with whom she got on very well by all accounts. This was because she herself was of itinerant stock, she told them – the McDonaghs were travelling people, just like themselves.

Frank's death did not diminish her imperious ways. When her eyesight was failing, Michael Rothschild was obliged to sit beside her at bridge, to point out which cards to play. This author and his wife would be occasionally ordered to bring her to lunch at Finnegan's in Dalkey. Diners at adjoining tables could sometimes be drawn into the conversation when points of political history or family connection could be discussed and argued about.

Trying, undoubtedly, but never boring or conventional and always, it has to be said, great fun, Moll Lemass died on 31 August 2001.

16.

The Modern Era

[Author's Note]: The minutes book of the Edward Yacht Club, which became the National Yacht Club in 1931, ends with the annual general meeting of 29 March 1969. Beyond that date, telling the club's story chronologically becomes something of an uphill job, principally because of fires and other misfortunes.

There is also the very sensible advice, when writing a history of any organisation, to stay away from modern times. For the historian to gain a proper perspective some detachment or distance from the subject is advisable.

Accordingly, what follows is of necessity an overview of how the club evolved since the 1970s, with occasional references to significant events and boats that sailed from the club during the period.

The photo below shows the rear elevation of the National Yacht Club as it was in 1963. The water, it will be noticed, comes up to the clubhouse wall. It's an interesting illustration of the fact that – up to that time – in all its essential features, the fabric of the building and its immediate surrounds had not altered much since John Cunningham built it.

All that was to change radically in the decades after 1970, when a balcony was added, various extensions were made to the forecourt, slipways extended and the pontoons that members are familiar with today added to the forecourt. In time a heavy-lifting crane was provided as well as a forklift truck for towing boats. (About the latter, there were initially some reservations – a fear, perhaps, that driver and truck would end up in the sea?)

The National Yacht Club, 1963

The impulse that prompted this surge of activity is that since the mid-1960s, boats had been growing both in number and size. This is clearly illustrated by the table at the end of this chapter. It relates to *all* boats racing regularly in the bay but it does reflect the fact that for all the waterfront clubs there was a trend that club committees would have to respond to. In 1963 there were 68 keelboats and 214 smaller craft racing in the bay; by 1975 the figures had increased sharply to 155 and 311 respectively.

Initially, most of the focus at the start of this period – the 1960s and 1970s – was on racing for dinghies and smaller craft such as Mermaids and Flying 15s. True, on the keelboat side, the number of Dragons was growing – they had reached 29 in 1975 – and there were valid claims that the Dublin Bay class had the highest number of boats in the world racing under the one club burgee. There was always a certain glamour attached to this class, and there still is, although in recent times numbers, sadly, have fallen away.

Looking back on the late 1960s, there is one dinghy event which some older members might have occasion to remember particularly well: it was the 505 Europeans in September 1969, hosted by the National Yacht Club (with the help of the RSGYC). This was the event that effectively put an end to the 505 class in Dublin Bay.

Owners probably knew it already but that series confirmed that to race competitively in that class internationally you must be prepared to spend a lot of money. None of the Irish competitors in that championship had the resources to make any headway against better funded rivals from abroad. Nor were they likely to have. Over the next year or so, a realisation grew that there were less expensive boats coming on the market that met their needs. And so, very soon, the 505 class quietly faded away in Dublin Bay.

For some, the obvious replacement was the Peter Milnes-designed Fireball, on the market since 1962. Over the years, many National Yacht club members have raced in this lightweight, pacy, not very expensive dinghy, its hull shape reminiscent of the American east coast Scow. They particularly liked its terrific downwind speed when planing, the ease with which it can be righted after a capsize, and the fact that its contour and hull shape lent itself to do-it-yourself fabrication. One National member, Roger Bannon, recalls having actually built *six* Fireballs when he raced in that class.

Roger Bannon, incidentally, could be classed as a serial boat owner and builder. By his own shocked admission, he owned *twenty-six* boats over his sailing career. In four classes – 420s, Flying Fifteens, Mermaids and J24s – he won ten national championships. His epic battle to introduce a GRP version into the Mermaids deserves a chapter to itself but that, alas, has to be left for another day.

See below Michael Chester's photo of Roger Bannon's *Dolly* and *Endeavour* during trials in 2004.

Do-it-yourself maintenance was in vogue in those years and many of the more senior sailors, out of war-time necessity, were manually more adept than the current generation. They also had the family garage to work in during the winter months, while most garages in suburban Dublin have long since been converted to domestic use.

Roger Bannon's Dolly *and* Endeavour

The late Sean Murray, the ESB's head chemist, was an avid Mermaid sailor and long-time National Yacht Club member who carried the do-it-yourself fashion to a new level when he persuaded fourteen ESB colleagues to combine and build not Fireballs, but GP14s in a disused ESB shed in Ringsend.

This was helped by the fact that the ESB chairman, Professor Charles Dillon, was also an avid sailor, and indeed something of a do-it-yourself man himself who had invented a self-tacking jib for his own cruiser, which he sailed out of the Royal Irish Yacht Club. The ESB's head carpenter cast an occasional professional eye on the work in progress, besides helping install the above-mentioned self-tacking jib. It's unclear whether all fourteen GP14s were actually built, but it certainly gave that class a certain boost in Dublin Bay.

Early Fireball recruits included the National's own Olympians, Johnny Hooper and Peter Gray. Two later NYC sailors, John Lavery and David O'Brien, carried off the Fireball World Championship in 1995. The class, for the reasons mentioned, expanded rapidly in Dublin Bay, far more so than was possible with the prestigious (and, of course, pricier, 505). In 1975 it had grown to 25 boats, sailed by prominent Dublin Bay sailors such as Brian and Peter Craig, Dick Felton, Paul Maguire, Howard Knott and Bob Curtis.

Many who later became prominent in waterfront club and race management looked back with some nostalgia on the years they raced with the Fireballs. Ronan Beirne, who runs the boat brokerage firm, Leinster Boats, and up to recently was Commodore of the National, was one; he also raced a Fireball in 1975, as did, it so happens, this author.

In the early 1970s one or two 505 sailors of sturdier physique found the newly-arriving Flying 15s more congenial. (These were not quite new on the scene, if you include David Newmark's wooden version which pre-dated the fibre-glass model on the NYC platform by some years.) To this observer, who was an NYC member at the time, the sudden appearance on the racing scene of the so many boats of that class all at once was almost miraculous.

A few months earlier, a lot of earnest hugger-mugger had been going on at the far corner of the NYC bar between the likes of Noel O'Hare, Teddy (Brian S.) Ryan, Sean Nolan and Arthur Lavery. And then, quite out of the blue it seemed, there sitting on the NYC platform was a fleet of new, shining Flying 15s. If it wasn't quite like that, as informed sources affirm, it is certainly the case that the arrival of the Flying 15s happened with unusual speed.

The catalyst was a small advertisement placed in the morning papers in October 1969 inviting people interested in forming a Flying 15 class to contact a given number. The notice emanated from Teddy Ryan, up to this time racing a GP14. From this came a series of meetings, and then discussions with John Godkin of Godkins Boats in Kinsale.

Six members indicated immediately that they were prepared to buy: Arthur Lavery, Michael Halpenny, Noel O'Hare, Sean Nolan, Dermot Ryan and Tony Neiland. Teddy Ryan agreed that he would purchase Bill Godkins' Flying 15 to make up the commitment of a minimum of seven boats for the 1970 season. John Godkin, the agent for Copeland, the favoured supplier of fibre-class Flying 15s at the time, accordingly placed an order for six boats. A marketing plan got under way immediately, a lot of wooden Flying 15s emerged from all quarters, and by the start of the 1970 season there were – astonishingly – *twenty-two* boats on the class roll.

Obtaining class status from DBSC, which was usually sceptical about claims about boat entry numbers from emerging classes, was no bother at all. It was granted at the June 1970 meeting and Larry Martin, the appropriate committee member at the time, was charged with providing racing facilities. The Flying 15s featured in the DBSC prize giving that year and have done so ever since.

By 1972 there were *thirty* Flying 15s on the DBSC roll, including Michael O'Rahilly's *Sionnach Rua*, which came second in the class championships that autumn on Lough Neagh. Not a bad performance for a class-newcomer against Ulstermen who had been racing Flying 15s from the early 1950s. The Flying 15s have continued to thrive on Dublin Bay ever since, mostly NYC-based boats. In

Michael O'Rahilly

2019 there were twenty-nine boats in the fleet including some very active veterans such as Ross Doyle, Michael McCambridge and Ronan Beirne, who crews alongside David Mulvin in a boat oddly called *Ignis Caput* (cod-Latin for 'fire ahead'.)

Possibly the most senior member racing a Flying 15 these days has to be Frank Burgess (second overall, Saturdays, 2019) who in 1972 was Class Captain of the Enterprises. This was another dinghy class, set up in the early 1960s by an NYC sailor, Neil Marr, which thrived into the 1970s until, inexplicably and most controversially, the DBSC committee of the day decided to withdraw its class status.

There had been talk of rationalisation of dinghy classes, the idea being that the GP14 had better development prospects than the Enterprise. Yet the latter was the second-largest class in the bay and there was an almighty row at the 1971 annual general meeting which resulted in a reprieve. But the word had gone out that the Enterprise's days were numbered in Dublin Bay, and at the end of the 1973 their class captain told the DBSC committee that in 1974 they didn't want a separate start and that, moreover, some of them were going off to widen their experience elsewhere. This wasn't a good idea at all.

There were other dinghy classes sailing out of the NYC in the 1960s and 1970s, such as 420s, Herons and Lasers. The 420s enjoyed a considerable popularity for a time with thirty-three racing in 1975. Many, if not most, were based in the National Yacht Club where a group of parents, which included Carmel Winkelmann and the late Paddy Kirwan, favoured the 420 as a step-up boat for juniors.

Sean Clune was an indefatigable promotor of the 420s. There are NYC members who still recall the arrival at the club of the first boats of that class. It happened after racing on a Thursday night and there was great excitement when a huge truck pulled up alongside the club wall and disgorged what seemed to be about a dozen 420s. Sean was in the middle of it all, supervising the unloading and no doubt enjoying all the publicity for the new class.

Dr Bernard Bolger, a local sailor, became national president of the class in 1979. He was one of the UCD research chemists who helped develop the Loctite glue and later Superglue. Unfortunately, the Americans who controlled the corporation, decided that they needed Bernard alongside them in Ohio and he had to leave Ireland and sailing behind for some years. He was, and still is, a gifted water colourist.

The 1970s were stressful times for flag-officers and their committees, not to speak of harassed boatmen who had the unenviable chore of trying to accommodate members clamouring for moorings. It was axiomatic that you didn't think of buying a keelboat unless you had somewhere to moor it – in fact, it still is. Boatmen became particularly alert to any news of members going cruising so that they could move some new keelboat owner on to the vacant mooring.

It was during Paul Johnston's term of office as Commodore (1969-1972) that the first step was taken to extend the platform space, aided, providentially, by infill coming from the recently-demolished Adelphi Cinema up the road. The extension was intended to provide parking for dinghies but, as was quickly realised, it could be used also to accommodate keelboats during the winter months, so furnishing an additional income stream. This it has done ever since, to no small advantage to the club's finances.

With larger boats, more and more members could now leave their customary inshore jousting and without trepidation set sail for other shores. John Hall, racing nowadays in Dublin Bay with his son Brian in the J109 *Something Else*, and very successfully too, has been competing in the Scottish series since 1984, missing only two years in all that time. Oddly, Tony Fox is the only other National sailor who has been disposed to race on the Clyde. True, Jim

John and Brian Hall's J109 Something Else *on the DBSC starting line.*
L to R: John Hall, Paddy Swords, Carolyn Thornton, Mikal Sanne,
Matt Paterson and Dave Egan.

Gorman, professionally a denizen of the high seas for much of his life, did indeed pass that way on a cruise to Norway but not to race. His navigation classes, it must be added, have been *de rigueur* for many years for members venturing off-shore. Jim's own most recent cruise has been a journey around the Aegean islands in *Helcia*, his Hans Christian 38.

The Mediterranean has always been favoured by National sailors. Michael (Sticks) O'Herlihy, before setting out across the Atlantic in *Evora*, recalled that much of his previous off-shore sailing had been in the Mediterranean.

One of the NYC's most intrepid of off-shore sailors has to be club's trustee, Cormac McHenry. Despite a busy professional life, Cormac has also been Hon. Secretary of the Irish Cruising Club, its Vice-Commodore and also its Commodore.

Cormac took *Ring of Kerry*, one of O'Brien Kennedy's 27 foot Kerry cruisers, single-handed to the Azores as well as on a number of other challenging cruises. Navigating the first of his Azores voyages in 1989 was by the old-fashioned way – sextant and compass; GPS had yet to come into general use. He was an inveterate single-handed sailor, totally on his own taking the Nicholson 31, *Erquy*, across the Atlantic in 1997. Later he acquired an American Island Packet 40 footer, *Island Life*, in which he and his wife Barbara nowadays cruise the Galician coast.

Going to the far side of the world, Conor O'Regan, Club Treasurer (2016-2020), took the family cruiser, *Pamina*, through the Panama Canal and down to the South Seas along with his wife, Henriet-

Ring of Kerry

ta, and for a time, his father Brendan – after some preliminary Aegean and Mediterranean cruising (see Sidelines section).

At the other extreme, Michael Madsen and his wife Ann, not too long ago, took their Sadlier 35, *Gabelle*, way north beyond the Arctic Circle to the Lofoten islands, and on to Svalbard, within 600 miles of the North Pole. Michael, it can be assumed, has Viking blood in his veins; his grandfather, was Danish.

The partnership of Peter Cullen and the late Martin Crotty favoured the Iberian coast, ultimately leaving their boat *Koala* in a Portuguese marina for much of the year. Martin Crotty, as well as Brian Barry, will always be associated with the club's biennial Dún Laoghaire to Dingle race for which he was the initial inspiration in 1995. This was not an easy jaunt by any means, as the number of retirals can sometimes testify. For some, it will always be a sort of Mecca, a journey you should undertake at least once in a lifetime.

Martin Crotty

Ida Kiernan

Others, like one-time club trustee Liam Shanahan, have preferred to go the full circle and compete in the Round Ireland Race (an experience, some have said, that gives their own local racing in Dublin Bay an additional allure).

Martin's Crotty's introduction to sailing was by a curious route, a sailing school organised by someone who up to now has been the National Yacht Club's sole woman Commodore, namely Ida Kiernan. (2000-2002). Ida's sailing school, the Dún Laoghaire Sailing Centre, based in 2 Roby Place in the basement the then-HQ of the Irish Yachting Association, was a great success, ending only when her business partner regretfully had to pull out. Alistair Rumball then stepped in to fill the void.

In retrospect, setting up a sailing school at the time was an extraordinary venture for a young woman still in her early twenties, 'shelving her safe and comfortable nine-to-five job in the civil service to make her living at the mercy of the truculent sea,' as an article about the project in the *Evening Herald* put in July 1977.

The need for such an undertaking had been impressed on Ida sometime in late 1972, perhaps after coming ashore in the Coal Harbour from an IDRA 14 when she was met by some parents asking how they could have their children taught to sail. The yacht clubs, of course, looked after the children of their own members and, anyway, courses were often over-subscribed. Supported by a credit union loan and with IYA backing, Ida and her sailing partner, Barry O'Loughlin, set about supplying the need with considerable zeal and self-assurance.

Initially, they had six Mirrors at their disposal, which rapidly grew to a fleet of twelve which included Mirrors (mostly) and some 420s as well as a small cruiser, a Sherriff (pronounced Sharif, as in Omar). There was also a panel of IYA-credited instructors, five of them women, and in winter months instructor Arna Dahm, normally resident in the Isle of Man, for navigation classes.

Ida and Barry showed considerable promotional flair in publicising their project, including a press reception in the Burlington where their well-thought out plans for the 1973 season were presented. In the centre of the room, set up on the Burlington's carpet, was an International 420. The press were impressed; Ida was described by one correspondent, Mary Lowry, as 'the youngest managing director' she had ever met.

There were visits to the principals of girls' schools in Dalkey and Glenageary, and for boys St. Michael's. They also canvassed the social clubs of local business houses, all of which had considerable effect. The Dún Laoghaire Sailing Centre thrived, bringing into sailing some later prominent NYC members such as Anita Begley and Ann McQuaid. The late and much missed Louis Smyth also came to sailing through Ida's sailing centre.

Ida's most notable sailing school pupil turns out to be someone who by virtue not only of her own attainments, which are considerable, but by those of her family has brought not a little fame and glory to the National Yacht Club. This is Cathy MacAleavey, born in Mexico, who was brought by her mother to Ireland when her father died unexpectedly. Her mother tried to have Cathy enlisted in the other Dún Laoghaire clubs but because of the regulations in force at the time was unsuccessful. The National, with eminent good sense and humanity, ignored the regulations and accepted her application, resulting in Cathy being able to sail there.

A Flying 15 start in a 2007 DBSC race

An early memory is of Cathy sailing a Laser in Dún Laoghaire Harbour, wearing cut-away jeans and crowned incongruously by a splendid hat. She was studying design in the Dún Laoghaire School of Art and Design in those days, which explains the hat. It may have been when she was training for the Seoul Olympics, for which she was one of the Irish team. Her husband is Con Murphy (NYC Commodore, 2006-2008) who, when he was in the Air Corps, piloted the Government jet. He and Cathy's involvement in the Olympic movement has brought a number of major international sailing events to the National and other Dún Laoghaire clubs.

Cathy's particular contribution to the National Yacht Club has been to junior sail training. Since the late 1960s, when Carmel Winkelmann and friends set up the Junior Section, its focus had been on teaching youngsters to sail and to get them used to the water, which accorded well with what parents and committees expected of it. With the passage of the years expectations evolved, and when Cathy took over the time was ripe was ripe to give junior training a more competitive edge. This policy has been a spectacular success and a number of Cathy's trainees and those of her successors have

Cathy and Con Murphy

been directed to Irish Sailing's training programme, bringing them to wider horizons on the international circuit.

There's no need to recall how all this influenced her own daughters' sailing careers. Claudine ultimately decided to put competitive sailing aside to concentrate on her medical studies and is now a children's doctor. And Annalise? Oh, Annalise, as the world and his wife knows, went on to Olympic glory in Rio in August 2016.

It was memorable occasion. Thousands from all of the Dún Laoghaire clubs crowded into the National to watch the final race on a giant television screen. There was almost a communal heart attack in the final moments as the boats raced toward the finishing line. And then, a place on the Olympic podium assured, moments of sheer unadulterated joy and delight as never before experienced in the old clubhouse. People hugged and wept, some who had spent years in competitive sailing were seeing at long last the reward of years' unremitting effort and the realisation of many dreams.

Curiously, Annalise's father was one of the people who had not witnessed his daughter's triumph. An international race officer,

An aerial view of the National Yacht Club

Con had most inconveniently been assigned to preside over the 49er Olympic race taking place at the same time. (Jack Roy, by the way, another NYC international race officer and President of Irish Sailing (2017-2020), the Irish sailing governing body, had performed a similar function at the previous Olympics.)

The homecoming to the National Yacht club on Thursday, 25 August, was equally ecstatic. Councillor Cormac Devlin presided over the official welcome in the People's Park. There were congratulory addresses from Shane Ross, Minister for Transport, Tourism and Sport and Mary Michell O'Connor, Minister for Jobs, Enterprise and Innovation. Commodore Larry Power presented Annalise with Honorary life membership of the Club. Annalise's coach, Rory Fitzpatrick, and sailing mentor, Sarah Winter (NZ) were also honoured. Club Manager Tim O'Brien and the catering staff hosted what has to have been the most memorable reception in the annals of the National Yacht Club.

DBSC's last Thursday night of the season had been cancelled, much to the disgruntlement of one member accustomed to arrive by plane for his Thursday night racing. To hold racing, however, would have been impossible. The guards had blocked off most of the Dún Laoghaire waterfront, launch services had been cancelled, and bar attendants had been borrowed from the other clubs to help meet the demands of the thirsty throng. Three television units were on the premises to record the event.

Finally, Annalise appeared around the corner of the Carlisle Pier, standing upright in a rib, bearing the Irish flag and surrounded by a flotilla of ribs carrying flares. As they approached the NYC pontoons, one member, with some historical perspective, noted that the scene suggested 'Queen Maeve in her chariot, leading the men of Éireann into battle'. Yes, indeed.

It was unforgettable moment. And where better to end this part of the chronicles of the National Yacht Club.

Annalise Murphy was welcomed home by a huge crowd at the National Yacht Club on 25 August 2016 after her achievement at the Rio Olympics.

Keelboats and Dinghies/ Light Craft Comparison

(Dublin Bay Sailing Club, 1963-2019)

Year	Keelboats	Nos.	Dinghies & Small Craft	Nos
1963	24 FTRS.	7	Enterprises	29
	CRs.1	23	IDRA14s	16
	Crs. 2	17	Fireflies	31
	21s	7	12 Ftrs	13
	Dragons	14	Wags	23
			Herons	31
			505s	15
			Mermaids	56
	Total	68	Total	214
1975	24 FTRS.	6	Fireballs	25
	CRs.1	23	IDRA14s	18
	Crs. 2	38	GP14s	25
	Crs 3	31	Fireflies	33
	21s	7	12 Ftrs	9
	Dragons	29	Sundries	10
	Glens	18	Wags	15
	Others	3	Lasers	14
	Total	155	Mermaids	36
			Flying 15s	24
	Total	155	Total	209

2019	Crs 0	7		IDRA14	9
	CRs.1	18		Wags	37
	Crs. 2	16		Lasers	44
	Crs 3	29		Mermaids	4
	Crs 5	29		Flying 15s	29
	31.7s	10		Fireballs	6
	Shipman	9		PY	11
	Ruffians	13			
	B211s	12			
	Glen	8			
	Sub Total	**(151)**			
	SB20s	13			
	Sportsboats	12			
	Grand Total	**176**		**Total**	**140**

May Day

MISCELLANEA

17.

Pyrotechnics

There is a current refurbishment of the club-house which includes a funky wet bar. This will feature the original beams
which are charred from a fire some year back – a club is not
a club without a fire or two, after all. – Gillian Nevin, *Sunday
independent*, 27 March 2005.

In their darkest moments, post-war National Yacht Club members
must have wondered whether some malignant fire demon was
stalking their clubhouse in those years, seeking an opportunity to
burn it down. There are no less than six recorded instances – of
varying degrees of severity – when fire threatened the existence of
the club.

The first actually happened the year the war broke out in the
summer of 1939. On 31 July, the *Irish Press* reported:

The National Yacht Club at Dún Laoghaire was threatened
by fire in the early hours of yesterday morning when flames
were noticed in an office. Dún Laoghaire fire-brigade succeeded in confining the fire to the office after half an hour's
work. Some shelving was destroyed and the interior was
damaged.

The second happened on 17 January 1949. 'A small outbreak', evidently, quickly put out by the fire brigade.

The third happened on 9 May 1953, causing considerable damage to the bar. The *Irish Press* reported that the local fire brigade had the fire under control in less than an hour.

The fourth sounds harmless enough, described on 30 January 1956 by Quidnunc of *The Irish Times*, as 'a cosy, small sort of fire', which was very quickly dealt with. None of the other newspapers mentioned it (Quidnunc knew about it because at the time he was very much enjoying himself sailing on one of the Dublin Bay Twenty Ones).

The fifth was on a different order of severity. Early on 27 May 1975, about 4.00 a.m., the Assistant Manageress, Bernadette Croofey, who was sleeping on the premises alongside her sister, Rita, was awoken by a loud bang, similar to that of an explosion. Fearing there might be an intruder, she brought her sister with her to investigate. When she got to the bottom of the stairs leading to the boathouse, she was nearly overcome by the smoke. After waking Mary Dougan, a waitress who was sleeping in another room, they got to a telephone and raised the alarm.

Thousands of pounds worth of sails and other boating equipment were destroyed or badly damaged in the blaze. Dún Laoghaire fire brigade was able to save a considerable part of the building but most of the premises suffered severe water damage. The fire was attributed to an electrical fault.

The sixth was the most serious of all, an out and out conflagration causing fears for the stability of the structure and disrupting plans for the 1984 season. Most inconveniently, it happened on the early morning of 5 June, just a week away from the commencement of the DBSC centenary celebrations, on which all of the waterfront clubs had been devoting much time and effort over the winter.

Not far off the mark was the *Evening Herald* headline of 5 June: '£150,000 blaze guts yacht club house'. Most of the damage, in fact, was internal. 'The main building is intact,' Freddie Cooney, who was the Club Commodore at the time, told the *Herald*, 'except for

Freddie Cooney

a hole in the roof made by firemen fighting the blaze.' Fortunately, no one was injured; Vera Farrell, the manageress, who lived on the premises was away for the bank holiday weekend. However, the fact that the club was empty at the time, and that the fire broke out about 2.00 a.m., meant that there was no one present to raise the alarm in good time or to rescue the club's collection of historic photographs and valuable paintings.

The Royal St. George Yacht Club was more fortunate during the fire that devastated that club's premises in 1919; there were people nearby with the presence of mind to rescue the club's treasured paintings, and equally important, the club records. Most of the National's records were lost in the 1984 fire apart from the minutes book of club's general meetings from 1902 to 1968 which, fortuitously, was on loan for research purposes at the time.

Older members will remember the intense activity of the committee, led by the Commodore, the late and ever lamented Freddie Cooney, in putting the club back on its feet in little more than a year. While the restoration was proceeding, the normal business of the club was carried on in a number of temporary buildings erected in the boat parking area. Winkie Nixon, who was writing a yachting column in the *Irish Independent* at the time, observed that it reminded members of a shanty town. No matter. It gave the committee and their advisors breathing space to look back and think hard about how they should proceed.

Providentially, among the club members was an architect, Fionán de Barra, who in response to a request from the Commodore at the time, Willie Maguire, had been already involved in preparing plans for a radical overhaul and possible extension of the clubhouse.

*'Another fine mess you got me into.' Paul Johnson and
Fionán de Barra inspect the boathouse damage.*

This is how Fionán recalls the years of 1984-1985:

Reinstatement and Improvement of NYC after Fire on 5th June 1984.

Early in 1983 I was engaged as architect by the National Yacht
Club Committee under Commodore William Maguire to survey the premises and prepare a report on necessary repairs
and improvements as well as possible means of extending
the building. Arising from this report, the Committee, now
under Commodore Freddie Cooney, decided to have all the
roofing replaced and to investigate the feasibility of connecting the building to the town main sewer. The original roof,

which had been built without any felt beneath the slates, was leaking in several places.

As was the case with all waterfront buildings at that time, all waste water from the Club discharged directly into the Harbour. On 6 May 1984 I submitted plans for a new sewerage system, with drains suspended beneath the Club and connected to a concrete holding tank below sea level, from which effluent would be pumped up to the main sewer on the far side of the railway.

Work on the new roof had just been completed, including asphalt on the central flat section, when the fire broke out on 5th June 1984. The building was unoccupied at the time and there was no fire alarm. The fire was noticed by a passerby in the small hours of Whit Monday morning. I received a phone call from Freddie Cooney at about 6.30 am and hurried to the Club to find the fire brigade still in attendance. I waited until the fire brigade had left and then entered the building. I climbed into the roof space and noticed that fire was still burning, low down, inside a stud partition.

I brought up an extinguisher and attempted without success to deal with this fire. I called the Garda on the footpath outside to summon the fire brigade to return and resumed my attempts at firefighting inside the roof space. Very soon an astonished fireman appeared beside me through the smoke and asked 'who are you?' 'I am the architect,' I replied and directed him to the top of the stud partition at ceiling level. He seemed to accept my presence as normal and directed his hose into the partition cavity and quickly extinguished what remained of the fire.

Later that day an emergency meeting of the Committee was held in the end of the dining room where the floor was sufficiently intact. All the upper floor at the bar end was completely destroyed. I gave a verbal report on the extensive damage and on 14 June 1984 I submitted a written report which was to form the basis of the subsequent insurance claim for reinstatement. The building was closed and arrangements were made to salvage as much of the contents as possible and erect temporary accommodation on the platform so that the Club could function somehow during the coming sailing season.

Taking down and removing damaged and dangerous ceilings, floors and partitions revealed the full extent of structural deficiencies and drainage problems that had been adverted to my report of 1983. I advised that since so much of the building and services required reinstatement, the Committee should avail of the opportunity to have a number of major improvements carried out that would be prohibitively expensive at any other time. I further advised that the cost of remedial works to comply with building bye laws and fire safety requirements that were not in force when the building was built, could now be claimed under the insurance policy.

And so, as Winkie Nixon wrote in the *Irish Independent*, 'the disaster was turned into a golden opportunity to make the club into a much more effective premises'.

In drawing up plans and specifications for the reinstatement of fire damage and development of the premises, I was ably assisted by John Egan, services engineer (and fellow NYC member) Noel Looney, structural engineer and Seamus McKenna, quantity surveyor. (I should also mention that throughout my involvement with the building, I had frequent meetings with the Trustees, Liam Boyd, Bob Kidney and Michael Kane, who were very understanding and supportive).

The total cost of the project was about £550,000, of which the insurers paid almost £300,000. The balance was funded by the members through a levy agreed at a special EGM, plans of the proposed improvements having been circulated to members by the Commodore, Freddie Cooney in October 1984.

After many meetings with the Committee, tenders were invited and a local contractor, Hobson Builders Ltd., was selected. The building contract was signed on 4th December 1984 and work started immediately on replacing the damaged roof so that further works could be completed under shelter.

View of ground floor and lower ground floor after 1984 fire

Work proceeded downwards and the bar was reopened twelve months after the fire. New concrete beams to carry the ground floor were held on temporary supports while major structural repairs were carried out to foundations in the sea bed during low tide. The building had been built on a series of granite piers and cast iron columns below sea level which supported heavy timber beams that carried masonry walls. Over time the ends of timber beams and roof trusses had rotted and compressed so that floors and roof had subsided by 50 mm on the seaward side.

Almost the entire lower floor was constructed of timber over the sea with a clearance of 1200 mm above high water. All timber beams, joists and flooring were replaced in concrete, using in situ beams to support precast inverted T beams with rigid foam insulation between them as permanent shuttering for a new reinforced concrete slab. The new concrete floor provided an opportunity to improve the toilets and shower layouts and install a completely new cast iron drainage system, suspended beneath the slab and connected to a concrete tank on the sea bed at the western end of the site. All effluent was then pumped through a 80 mm diameter pipe to the main sewer on the far side of the railway. A manhole was constructed outside the eastern end of the building with a suitable invert level to enable the building to be extended eastwards in the future to provide new changing rooms, showers etc with a roof terrace opening from the bar for which I prepared sketch plans at the request of the Commodore, Freddie Cooney.

In reflecting on my long association with the Club premises, I feel that the most significant improvement that was carried out during that time was the installation of a proper drainage system that replaced the 100 year old practice of dumping all sewage and waste water from the Club into the Harbour, untreated.

Another notable improvement was the new bar counter and service lift which were installed after the 1984 fire. Many visitors today believe the bar counter, with hand carved details, dates from the nineteenth century.

18.

The Protest Room

For generations now, protests arising from incidents during racing in Dublin Bay have been held in the National Yacht Club's dining room. There is a reason for this. Most racing in the bay is organised by Dublin Bay Sailing Club, which draws its committees and race management teams from all of the Dún Laoghaire waterfront clubs. The Royal Irish Yacht Club is where the keelboat race management teams meet before racing for coffee and consultation, the Royal St. George provides berthing spaces for DBSC ribs, and the Dún Laoghaire Motor Yacht Club was where racing results, up to recent times, were processed.

The National Yacht Club's contribution – in the interest of intra-club symmetry, you might say – was to put aside the dining room for meetings of the DBSC protest committee on Monday evenings.

A number of National Yacht Club members have made notable contributions to this activity. The late Dr. John Donnelly, a UCD academic and a prize-winning dinghy sailor before he moved into keelboats, was the local Protest Secretary for many years and then became a highly respected international race judge. In later years, the much missed Paul Murphy presided, with customary panache, over many a closely-argued protest in the NYC dining room before he was appointed a national race judge. The late Ray Duggan, too, in recent times, had been a very effective Protest Secretary. And, of course, Tom Mulligan as well. On the international scene, NYC member Ken Ryan officiated at two Americas Cup series, as jury member in 1983 and as jury chairman in 1987, not to mention a distinguished career in the administration and development of international racing.

Protest Committee hearings, for those unfamiliar with yacht racing, are akin in some respects to a Steward's Enquiry in horse racing. It decides which boat has infringed the rules and how scores should be adjusted. Damages are not its province although Learned Friends who participate have been known to make Law Library jokes about 'looking for costs'.

It's all quite forensic, a judicial affair, and if conducted strictly according to the rules laid down in the International Rules of Sailing, its findings can be accepted in a court of law. Given the furious outbursts that occur regularly during racing, proceedings can be surprisingly calm and good-humoured.

One Dublin Bay sailor of forty years' experience confessed that he had avoided protests all his life because he expected them to be a continuum of the fractious arguments he had already experienced out on the water. Eventually obliged to attend a hearing, he was so delighted with the consideration and politeness with which he was treated that he was almost tempted to move a vote of thanks to all concerned.

And the late Brian Grant, a veteran of many protests, once appeared in the protest room carrying a tray of drinks, for all the world as though the proceedings were just a continuation of an interesting discussion he had been having in the bar. Brian was a major a figure in the advertising world where, at the time, a round of drinks was a customary aid to fluency in business dealings. Perish the thought, but there was no suggestion that on this occasion he was attempting to bribe the committee.

Drink seems to have featured quite a lot in many waterfront anecdotes. On one occasion, during a power strike, hearings were conducted in near darkness, the only illumination coming from a couple of candles stuck in two empty wine bottles. The first protest on the schedule went on interminably, for almost two hours it seemed, until the protestee conceded that, having listened carefully to the evidence of his crew, he now concluded that he was in the wrong.

The parties to the following protest were two Mermaid sailors, the late Eustace Dockery and – recollections differ – but it may have been the late Gay Brennan or Gerry O'Neill. Needless to say, when the pair appeared in the protest room, having been alone in the nearly darkened bar for the best part of two hours, they were both, as the phrase goes, adequately refreshed. Eustace, who had a bad stammer, showed none of it on this occasion, addressing the hearing with great fluency. Asked at the end of his evidence to summarise his arguments, instead of the customary recital of the rules infringed, he launched into a most stirring exhortation finishing with what he said was a quotation from Psalm 153.

After the parties left the room, there was an impressed silence. It was broken by one of the committee observing drily, 'I wish to point out, Mr. Chairman, that there is no such thing as Psalm 153. They end at 150.' Which goes to show that, in the presence of sailors of that era, you misquoted scripture at your peril. Eustace lost his protest.

During the war years, it is said that he was in charge of an anti-aircraft battery guarding Buckingham Palace. Eustace had particular trouble with words starting with F and when one day a German bomber appeared overhead he tried to give the appropriate signal ('Fire'). 'F---f---, F---f---' he called out uselessly. And then, as the bomber circled around unharmed and departed, he added, 'Don't worry. We'll f*****ng well get him next time.' The f*****ng word – a word with which Eustace had no difficulty at all – became known in Ireland at one time as the Garrison Adjective.

Gay Brennan, mentioned above, was a member of the National Yacht Club, Dublin Bay Sailing Club and at one time a president of the Mermaid Sailing Association. A competitive sailor, he won many trophies over a sailing career of forty years or more and enjoyed the esteem and regard of the Dún Laoghaire sailing community. He was also a successful businessman, a director of the family insurance firm, Brennan Insurances and, though called to the Bar, didn't practice until late in life.

Gay's first boat was the Mermaid *Betsan*, which he raced for some years with Donard O'Doherty. From 1986, with the one-time DBSC Rear-Commodore Jonathan O'Rourke, he raced his beloved *Tiller Girl*. Saturday racing for Gay, Jonathan recalled on the occasion of his death, was invariably preceded by a round of golf in Milltown and followed by a Gordon and Schweppes in the National Yacht Club. He also enjoyed going on winter skiing holidays into his seventies.

He particularly relished the occasional jousting of the protest room and reputedly never lost a protest. Protest secretaries loved having Gay on their committees. Besides being extremely knowledgeable about the sailing rules, he was great company and, as chairman of many hearings, well able to deal with argumentative or unruly characters.

There was something of the old-style Dublin Bay sailor about Gay. Sailing was important but so also were the formalities, the etiquette, the rituals of the sailing world.

One notable encounter was Gay's clash with another prominent member of the Dún Laoghaire sailing community who like himself was a member of the legal profession. The protestor, for some reason, failed to turn up so Gay then turned to the solicitor, who was the protestee, saying, 'Mr. So-and-So, I call on you to give us your evidence.'

The protestee, very sensibly and perfectly within his rights, said he had no evidence to give.

'Mr. So-and-So,' demanded Gay, 'I call on you to give your evidence.'

Again, a polite refusal.

'Mr. So-and-So,' said Gay, 'I call on you to give us your evidence.'

Still no response.

'Mr. So-and-So,' said Gay in a voice of thunder, 'I call on you to *withdraw.*'

Then, when the protestee had departed, Gay turned to the rest of the committee and murmured, 'God, how I *hate* solicitors'. Which was not true at all.

Then there was the occasion when Gay, on the other side of the table, so to speak, produced with a flourish and in Irish his first witness, who was prominent in Irish language circles. The chairman, vaguely sensing that there was some gamesmanship involved in all this, played along and offered to have the witness give her evidence in Irish, translating it if required. The offer was gracefully refused, much to the relief of the other members of the committee who were becoming alarmed at the way things were going. A pity, it was thought afterwards. It would have been a notable first to have a Dublin Bay protest heard in what Gay himself might have called the mellifluous tongue of the Gael.

Gay was much missed, firstly by his family, and also by the many friends in Dún Laoghaire and the National Yacht Club who enjoyed his company and who shared his love for the sea. His obituary on the Dublin Bay Sailing Club web site quoted aptly the Dingle boatman, 'ní bheidh a leithéid arís ann'.

On another occasion one of the parties to a protest was a judge of the High Court. The Protest Secretary reasoned that in fairness to the other party it would be well to have a couple of senior lawyers on the protest committee who would not be fazed by the judge's eminent knowledge of jurisprudence. Unfortunately, some lawyers, when approached, thought for a bit and said on reflection, 'better not'. One particular solicitor did not refuse, however, saying that he would serve on that committee if it was the last thing he did. That was Seymour Cresswell (the elder) who was very ill at the time and in fact died a few weeks later.

The protest hearing proceeded without incident. At one point, when asked if he had a witness, the Judge rose to fetch him, at which the Protest Secretary intervened helpfully, 'ah, don't bother, sure I'll fetch him'. His Lordship looked up sharply, quite undeceived by this show of amiability. He recognised full well that its purpose was to prevent him giving his witness some last minute coaching.

He was, nevertheless, quite impressed by the way things were conducted at the hearing. After proceedings had concluded – His Lordship lost, having been judged to have been plainly barging on the starting line – he remarked on the way out to the Protest Secretary: 'You know, you have a very good system of litigation here in Dublin Bay.' Which pleased everyone no end.

Lawyers, as you might expect, are very useful people to have on a protest committee. On one occasion, the hearing was dragging on endlessly – beyond midnight, in fact – and there was no sign that the chairman could wind things up. The lawyer – afterwards an eminent member of the judiciary – resolved the matter very smartly.

'Mr Chairman,' he said, looking at his watch, 'this hearing was scheduled to take place on a given date. It is now past twelve o'clock, the following day. I would suggest that the proceedings could be deemed illegal.' Whether this was true or not, the hint was taken and the Chairman, to everyone's relief, seized the opportunity and postponed continuing the hearing until another evening.

Having a good chairman at a protest hearing matters. As can sometimes happen, during one particular hearing it emerged that there was a flaw in the committee's proceedings, a fault seized upon with relish by the protestee. 'Even if I were at fault,' he told them triumphantly 'you can't do anything about it because this committee is illegally constituted.' This was true enough because the race was a joint Royal Alfred–DBSC affair and the committee, of course, should have made up of members of both clubs, which it wasn't.

As the committee ground its teeth in frustration the Chairman, Willie Maguire, as it happened, Commodore of the NYC at one time, solved the problem. 'Mr So and So,' he enquired, fixing the culprit with a steely glance, 'is this conduct proper to a member of a *Corinthian* yacht club?'. The effect was most gratifying (although some members of the committee wondered whether the miscreant actually understood the meaning of the word). He sat up, reflected a bit – and thinking perhaps of all sorts of unpleasant letters directed to his club's Commodore – conceded that perhaps he was in the wrong and in the circumstances thought it best to retire from the race.

Things do not always proceed peacefully. There was an occasion when all of thirty boats had protested to the Race Officer for some fault aboard the committee vessel. They weren't all expected to turn up but the Protest Secretary, nevertheless, judged that it was likely to be tumultuous meeting. He decided that it would be advisable to have as chairman someone well experienced in dealing with argumentative groups. His choice fell on the CEO of a big construction firm who, he judged, by virtue of having presided over many contentious site meetings, had all the experience needed. The rest of the committee shared his view and they were not mistaken.

The meeting started initially as the secretary had predicted, with much cross-talk and interruptions, without much progress being made. The chairman let it all run for a minute or two and then pounced.

'Mr. So and So,' he said icily to the protester who was trying to dominate the meeting. 'Did I ask you to speak?'

'No, but as I was saying …'

'Mr. So and So, do you hear me,' thundered the chairman, 'did *I ask you to speak?'*

'No, not exactly…'

'Mr So and So,' said the chairman,' you will speak when I ask you to. *Is that understood?'*

Yes it was and everyone else present, all suddenly struck silent by this stark display of executive power, nodded in agreement.

The way protests are conducted hasn't changed much over the years. True, when a lady enters the protest room nowadays to give evidence, the committee no longer stands up respectfully. This was the practice certainly up to the 1980s. Asked about it recently, one young woman produced a damning verdict on this genteel behaviour of earlier generations: 'It would not be thought *cool.'*

Ah well, *tempora mutantur nos et mutamur in illis,* as earlier generations would have had no trouble in saying.

19.

The Junior Section –
How It Came About

Carmel Winkelmann remembers.

In order to keep alive for future generations of club members the incredible story of its Junior Section's beginnings, I will give you a brief outline of how it came about. My memory may not be exact, but allow a little license to an old lady's thoughts, because the important parts are accurate.

Chapter One begins when a young (just married, I believe) Irishman, who was in Denmark representing his country, spotted a number of small boats

Carmel Winkelmann

with equally small children sailing them. He made enquiries and was introduced to Paul Elvstrøm, known as the Mozart of Sailing, one of the greatest sailors ever, who was responsible for introducing the sport to young Danish sailors. They became lifelong friends until Paul's death last December. Paul introduced the young Irishman to the *Optimist* – for that was the little boat he had seen – and Paul arranged for the Irishman to get its plans. The young Irishman was Johnny Hooper, who with Peter Gray at Naples in 1960 were the first Irish sailors ever to win an Olympic race.

Johnny came back to his club, the National Yacht Club, and, fired up with thoughts of starting a junior section, asked the then Vice-Commodore could he do so. He was told there was no room. He persisted and after a number of weeks, with the blessing of the then Commodore, John McConnell, and the evolving interest of the Vice Commodore, Paul Johnston, it was agreed he could go ahead in a small area outside the boat house.

At this stage a number of parents became more than a little interested and boats were built in garages and basements of houses. In May 1967 The Baby was born and the parent was Johnny Hooper. He formed a committee of Dads, and it fell to us Mums to set about teaching the children with a loud hailer while sitting on Bob Kidney's boat and that awful Irish Lights barge. I can still smell the creosote and Seagull droppings. That was all the equipment we had.

Things got better and it was decided to build a wooden platform to the west of the boathouse to house the children and their boats. BUT, and it was a big but, where was the money to come from to build it? By now Paul Johnston was Commodore. He and Vice-Commodore Liam Boyd called a meeting of the parents to see if they had any fund raising ideas. I got a dig in the ribs from Bernie Hooper who whispered, 'tell him we will run fund raising events'. Like an idiot, I stood up and said we would get x numbers of pounds, and hoped the committee would match it. This was rather embarrassing as my husband was just about to become Hon. Treasurer of the club.

In any event, we ran a Christmas fare of items made by us mothers. Bernie still has a Christmas stocking made by Barbara Kirwan. Pat Douglas made Christmas floral decorations and Maura Mc-Grath corralled people to visit our fare. We were on our way.

Each year we ran a Dutch auction which became famous for a dreadful pottery flowerpot which Mildred Mooney, Pat Douglas's mother-in-law, had brought back from a visit to Portugal. It was brought back each year for sale and the bidding for this ghastly object was frantic to the point where one year it fetched £30.00 almost the cost of an Optimist fully rigged. We got the platform built.

Our October Adult Optimist and Mirror Derbys became legion and we raised money for our kitty and, with membership fees charged for the children, we advanced to being able to employ instructors like Peter Craig, Rupert Jeffares for half days until we got our own full time instructors, Robert Dix, Sheila Treacy, John Blaney and the late Lee Cuff Smith.

It was great fun this year to see some of our former juniors of fifty years ago, some of whom are now grandfathers, sail again in an Optimist Derby. I could at this stage deviate and mention the formation of the East Coast Committee since by now the Royal St. George Yacht Club, with Elizabeth Jameson in charge, the Royal Irish Yacht Club with John McFarlane and most clubs on the north and south sides had started junior sections under the banner of the IYA.

After a few years Johnny handed the baby to a committee of NYC parents and with the help of Arthur Lavery, Paddy Kirwan, Don Douglas, Peter Grey, Michael Halpenny, Pat Duffy and many more Dads but especially Don and Peter. Formal instruction was put on the programme. I actually have the book we kept with all the children's names in it – the year they passed the various tests and stages. It is an interesting record, which the club should have.

Thus the format for the IYA Junior programme was born and the baby became a toddler. Peter Gray brought that toddler to a teenager when he was Chairman of the IYA Junior Committee and then as President. Irish sailing owes Johnny Hooper an enormous debt as it was his dream, foresight and tenacity that built a pyramid which has resulted in this club producing local, regional, national, European and World Champions such as our world champion, John Lavery. The NYC followed John's, Peter's and Michael's footsteps in sending some amazing people to represent Ireland at the Olympic Games, cumulating in Annalise's silver medal.

There are many more chapters to the book but without the first chapter there would be no book. The Junior Section gave us parents the wonderful gift of lifelong friendships. This club, us parents and children owe Johnny Hooper an enormous debt and he gave me over fifty years of helping in the sport I love.

20.

The Billiards Room

The event, referred to handily as The Preston Ball is not – as the uninitiated might believe – an actual ball but in fact a snooker tournament that takes place over the sailing off season, the high points being the auction, which takes place on the third Friday in January, and the final contest, which takes place on the Friday before the boat launching in April.

It ranks high in the National Yacht Club's social programme. If you attend, you must come in black tie and be possessed of a sound constitution such as might be required for a rugby club social. It is not for persons of a sensitive disposition. Ladies do not attend. The only recorded instance of a woman attending was when Miss Ida

Kiernan was Commodore. That was probably ex-officio and, anyway, Ida Kiernan, an experienced Mermaid sailor and a one-time boss of a sailing school, would have been well able to deal firmly with any difficult situation that might arise.

The tournament is called after an eminent medical practitioner, Dr Charles Preston Ball, whose name, unfortunately, has unusual associations in the sailing world – a dreadful family tragedythat transfixed Dublin society in 1936. The sad event has been dealt with in a number of publictions and on television and hardly requires recapitulation: suffice it to say that Ball's son, Edward, had a serious mental condition which caused him, in a fit of rage, to kill his mother, Lavinia, and deposit her body in the sea at Shankill. It was never recovered. In the subsequent trial, the jury found Edward guilty but insane.

Sean Hooper SC, member of the Edward Ball defence team

Mrs Ball's brothers were involved in the Dublin Bay sailing scene. Edward Weatherill (born 18 March 1887) joined Dublin Bay Sailing Club in 1912, when he was nominated for membership of DBSC by Charles Inglis Moore who, with his brother James, raced the 21 footer, *Oola*. It's not unlikely that Edward crewed on *Oola* before he enlisted in the Royal Dublin Fusiliers on the outbreak of war.

This did not have a happy outcome. Promoted first sergeant, he was 2nd lieutenant, B Company, 7th Battalion, when he was killed in the fighting at Suvla Bay, Gallipoli on 15 August 1915. The 7th Battalion was one of the 'pals' battalions, the 'pals' in Edward's case being members of the Monkstown and Lansdowne Football Club. He was undoubtedly a brave man. He was credited with saving five men at Suvla Bay the morning he was killed.

The record is unclear, but Edward Weatherill was probably a member of the Edward Club, just like his brother Archie (recte

Archbold Mackenzie Weatherill), Lavinia's elder brother who, according to the minute book, attended Edward Yacht Club meetings up to 1920. Archie seems to have moved around a bit. In August 1922, in his capacity as consul for both Portugal and Norway, he attended the funeral of President Arthur Griffith. In 1936, a month or two after Lavinia's death, he relinquished the position of Honorary Consul for Japan in favour of another member of the shipping fraternity, Major J. Hollwey, who had recently retired from the Royal Field Artillery and taken charge of the family firm, G. Bell & Co.

And the Preston Ball snooker championship? For its origins we have to rely on club lore – there is no other record. Legend has it that after the trial, the Doctor felt he ought to resign his membership of the National Yacht Club. His friends thought otherwise. They felt he was in no way to blame, went to his home and – so the story goes – marched him to the Club and forced him to withdraw his resignation.

The Doctor regained his equilibrium, resumed his practice, and married the nurse, Violet, who looked after his surgery. The club minutes record him attending annual general meetings; on one occasion they record him speaking in favour of that perennial – a motion to increase club subscriptions.

The Preston Ball snooker championship is a complicated affair, the finer details of which are beyond the scope of this work. First, the names of members who have entered for the championship are drawn from a hat. Later there is an auction, presided over by a member of notable fluency and robust temperament. Ability to command the room is an essential requirement (the present incumbent is Brian Mathews). Bids are effectively bets on the known handicap of the member concerned. Sometimes bids reach considerable levels where a contestant of high repute might be involved or syndicates formed.

Finally, a list of contestants is compiled. Based on this list, a series of a contests take place, with a reducing number of contestants – 64, 32, 16, 8, 4, 2. The final contest traditionally takes place on the Friday before the boat launching in April. Contestants, incidentally, are allowed to bid on themselves up to a stated proportion, 50 per cent until lately.

Some great names in the snooker world have played on the NYC billiard table. Among them is Alex (Hurricane) Higgins who, it is said, was defeated by a local NYC champion, George Morosini Whelan, who was associated with a famous dance school. Local champions have included Michael Kane, Flick Hardy, Corry Buckley and Tom Donnelly of Green Spot Whiskey. And, of course, Mr. O.G. McWilliams, who presented the McWilliams trophy.

Billiard players and sailors have not always seen eye to eye. There were some recriminations at the 1955 annual general meeting about the Twenty Ones being unable to hold their class dinner on one particular evening because precedence had been accorded to a snooker dinner. The committee, it was stated, had based their decision on the fact that the snooker players were all members of the NYC, which was not so in the case of the Twenty Ones, who could come from any club. This raised the ire of some, like M.M. (Mickey) D'Alton, who claimed there was a danger that the NYC was becoming a snooker club.

Billiards or snooker have been played in the clubhouse from the club's early days. In 1872 local newspapers carried an advertisement from the Club Steward (George Smith) looking for a billiard marker. There were many such advertisements in those years, some of which laid stress on the need for applicants to be honest and sober. Why honesty and sobriety should be so essential is unclear. Could it be because some billiard markers – young people usually who kept the score and fetched the drinks – might be susceptible to bribery or their integrity undermined by drink?

It is good to note that George Smith's advertisement carried no such stipulation.

Snooker Stalwarts

Michael Rothschild

John Loughrey presents special trophy to Barry O'Sullivan for thanks for his Chairmanship of Snooker Committee

A youthful Chris Johnston when long locks were in fashion.

Hubert Kearns

John (known, unaccountably, as the Goo) Maguire,
of the Maguire sailing dynasty

The late and ever-missed Dr. Ronnie O'Donovan

George Morosini Whelan, a 24 class sailor and an
NYC champion, who defeated world champion
Alex (Hurricane) Higgins in an exhibition match

21.

Club Development, 1998-2007

Forecourt Extension

The final years of the twentieth century and the early years of the millennium are justly regarded in Ireland as a period of excess and uncontained economic exuberance. For the National Yacht Club, no less than for the other Dún Laoghaire clubs, the record is markedly more positive; it was an era when, after years of restraint, the club committees were able to embark on a programme to deal with some long outstanding facilities and clubhouse issues.

The first to be dealt was the forecourt area, which was clearly inadequate. There simply wasn't enough space to store members' boats during the winter months. And during the summer season there were no facilities to lift boats for scrubbing, or to provide for keelboat dry sailing, a growing trend; boats couldn't come alongside the quay because there wasn't enough depth of water there.

To scrub your boat you had to secure it to the eastern side of the forecourt, beside the old lifeboat (Coopers') slip where there was a tall crane (if you wanted your mast lifted in or out). This was tide-dependent. Also, there wasn't enough space for dinghies, which could be awkward during national and international events. The two slipways were too narrow and there wasn't enough turning space at the top level.

On 3 March 1997 the Department of the Marine relinquished control of Dún Laoghaire Harbour in favour of a new semi-state harbour board. Barely seven months later the new board was able to present to the Dún Laoghaire Rathdown County Council a planning application for a marina of 680 berths. It signalled a new approach to the management of the harbour which, with the exception of the Carlisle and Ferry Piers, was very much as John Rennie had visualised it in the early nineteenth century.

The response of the National Yacht club was equally prompt and decisive: the establishment of a subcommittee to plan the development of its water front and forecourt area. (Clubhouse enhancement, a subject already much argued about, was to be considered at a later stage. A plan for a mini-marina in the Carlisle Basin was not pursued.) The subcommittee was fortunate in having as its chairman Ged Pierse, who had a professional background in major construction projects, and as technical advisor Roger Cagney, of Kirk McClure Morton, consulting engineers.

The plans for forecourt enlargement were agreed to by the members at an EGM on 2 November 1998. As might have been anticipated, there were some objections to spending money on the project. What seems to have carried the day was an interjection from former Commodore Michael Horgan: 'if you don't proceed with this, the National will be the backwater of the Dún Laoghaire clubs' (the point being that the other two major clubs had already undertaken renewal and expansion programmes). In retrospect the funding arrangements don't appear to have been too onerous – partly from bank borrowing, partly from reserves, and partly from a members' contribution of €600 spread over six half-yearly periods.

With initial hurdles overcome, the project proceeded apace. Given the scale of what was involved, progress was remarkable by any measure. Fortunately, Charles Brand, the forecourt contractor, was more or less already *in situ*, having just finished a similar job in the Royal St. George. This had a beneficial effect on the price quoted for the NYC job and allowed the job to progress more expeditiously.

There were a few hiccups. First there was the matter of the club crane. The intention had been to move it from the northeast edge of the forecourt adjoining the old lifeboat (Coopers') slip to a new position facing northwards on forecourt extension, thus allowing it to be used at all stages of the tide. Examination of the crane detected an ominous crack in the base and defects in the mast which put an end to that idea; closer examination led to the decision that it would have to be de-commissioned.

Happily, Ged Pierse, with his numerous construction involvements, was able to lay hands on a splendid heavy duty replacement which, very generously, he presented free of charge to the club. The only cost was an extra metal base to raise its lifting height and the provision of an additional piling under the crane site to support the weight of both crane and lifted boats.

Another problem found during the construction of the forecourt was sinkage of the eastern section of the existing platform. The gravel under the concrete slabs was found to be leeching out at the seaward edge. The solution was to pump concrete into the voids. Extra costs were incurred as a result but it was thought to be necessary at the time.

Nevertheless, despite these distractions and some other issues, the project was virtually complete at the end of May 1999. Throughout this period, the Harbour Board had helpfully provided winter storage for the club's keelboats on the Carlisle Pier. The seasonal lift-in took place on 30 April, not much later than usual.

With the completion of this project, the club's usable forecourt area had increased from 1400m² to about 2,250m² – a two-thirds increase. Independently of the tide, with two metres at low water springs, boats could now be lifted out at any time for scrubbing and dry sailing by Ged Pierse's magnificent 10 ton crane. Much protection for this operation is afforded by the new L-shaped breakwater (supplier, SF Marina Systems, Goteborg, Sweden) which when linked to the existing pontoon provided a splendid pool where club launches and ribs could moor (Mermaids, too, to compensate for the loss of their moorings). On race days some boats could now come alongside the breakwaters to collect crews, so relieving pressure on the ever-busy launch service.

For the Commodore and officers who oversaw the project (Commodore Barry McNeaney, Vice-Commodore Ida Kiernan, Rear Commodore Chris Moore, Hon. Treasurer, Paul Fallon, and Hon. Secretary, the late and ever-lamented Michael Bolger) it was a busy period and not without its stressful moments. But also something to look back on with much satisfaction – the largest expansion of the club's platform since its beginnings in 1870.

Barry McNeaney

Clubhouse Refurbishment, 2004-2007

By Con Murphy

- Commodore, 2002-2005, Chris Moore; Vice Commodore, 2002-2004, Ken Slattery; Vice Commodore, 2004-2005, Con Murphy; Commodore, 2005-2008, Con Murphy; Vice Commodore, 2005-2008, Peter Ryan.

- Development Committee, 2004-2008, Con Murphy, Terry Rowlands, Freddie Cooney, Ken Slattery, Chris Moore, Peter Ryan. Finance Committee, Con Murphy, Larry Power, Andrew Mackey, Ken Slattery.

- Planning Permission granted 26 June 2003; Applicant: National Yacht Club

- Development: Construction of a single storey extension housing changing-room facilities and ancillary accommodation; extended bar area and office to rear; replacement of stair to balcony; modification of door and window openings to rear and NW elevations; internal refurbishment of original building; replacement of existing and provision of new air handling equipment and ancillary ductwork and works to front site (protected structure) at National Yacht Club.

At an EGM in late 2003 a €2.2 million redevelopment 'finishing the job' was proposed. The motion passed by a small majority so the committee announced that they would not go ahead with the proposal.

Chris Moore

At the AGM in March 2004, Commodore Chris Moore announced that the committee would come back to members with revised development and refurbishment plans that would commence on 1 September 2004 and revised funding proposals.

Con Murphy was elected Vice-Commodore and immediately started discussions with David Crowley of Architects Cantrell Crowley to reduce costs from €2.2 million to €1.7 million.

Apart from the pressing need to redevelop the club, the outstanding fees of approximately €200,000 that would have been payable on top of the outstanding platform loan of €260,000 if the development did not go ahead, was a strong incentive for the Committee.

An EGM was held on 28 June 2004 at which a presentation from Con outlined the challenges facing the club, its future requirements and the aims of the proposals. Changes from original proposal included a significantly cheaper/better value (€.5 million), individual donations reduced from €2,000 to €1,200, an option to pay by instalments over two years, the tax claim optional, not mandatory, increased borrowings , no kitchen facility downstairs, no bar extension under the platform and the deletion of the duty boatman's office near the top of the slipway. The development would include a multipurpose room/wet bar on lower ground floor, better and more modern changing rooms, appropriate staff facilities (offices/dining/boathouse), new boathouse facilities, a refurbished dining room/bar and hallway, a dedicated race/event management accommodation, wheel chair access, an upstairs toilet and additional ladies toilets and better access to the club. The three motions were approved:

1. Proceed with refurbishment and extension of the clubhouse at a cost of €1.7 million.

2. Members agree to donate €1,200 each.

3. Committee authorised to take out a mortgage of €1.2 million.

The contractors CLG started on site on Monday, 6 December 2004 under a fixed price contract for €1,411,620. The new changing rooms were opened for use just in time for the inaugural Dún Laoghaire Regatta which ran from Thursday, 7 July to Sunday, 10 July.

At the EGM in November 2005, a motion to increase borrowings from €1.2 million to €1.6 million was approved. This was due to the builder's contract price of €1.4 million increasing to €1.5 million due to extras, the original estimate of €200,000 for the refurbishment of the upstairs area of the club being increased to €300,000 to allow for a more comprehensive refurbishment and provision of replacement furnishings, a shortfall in member's donations, and a lower yield (€120,000) than originally envisaged (€240,000) from the tax refund scheme availed of by the club.

The redevelopment and refurbishment, completed by early 2007, transformed the club and was considered by all to have been a great success. The new world class modern facilities ensured the successful hosting of the 2007 Laser 4.7 European Championships, the 2008 Laser SB3 World Championships and many other major events since.

SIDELINES

22.

Founding Members Jerome and Richard O'Flaherty

There were two Dr O'Flaherties, Jerome and Richard, father and son. Both were licentiates of the Royal College of Surgeons of Ireland. Jerome, the son of an army surgeon, had married Sarah Studdert, one of the Studdert family of Bunratty Castle. The two Dr O'Flaherties, on 26 November 1869, attended that seminal meeting in the Anglesey Arms Hotel which resulted in the establishment of the Kingstown Royal Harbour Boat Club (which became in due course the National Yacht Club). Jerome took charge of the meeting after John Crosthwaite, TC, had vacated the chair.

Richard was a keen sailor and yachting correspondents used to refer to him familiarly as 'the Doctor'. One such correspondent, in a sort of *jeu d'esprit*, imagined in a *Yachting World* article the sort of subjects that the Doctor and his friends talked about while they lunched one Sunday aboard J.M. Ross Todd's *Comus* in Kingstown Harbour – 'the merits of a water-colour by a well-known marine artist … and a few such weighty subjects as the congested districts and the towns of Gt .Britain and Ireland, the advantages arising from free education, the Russian drama and its effects on English morals etc'.

It's not known whether his father, Jerome, also sailed but he certainly contributed to the debenture scheme that raised the initial £2,000 to build the clubhouse. You can see his name on the debenture certificate displayed on the wall as you go downstairs in the clubhouse, as well as his address, 101 Upper Georges Street, which is where the O'Flaherties had their dispensary.

As dispensary doctors – though at different times – they became *ex-officio* sanitary inspectors for the borough. This required them to report on sanitation conditions in the town. Jerome's reports on what he was finding were frank and unsparing; they were quoted in evidence before the Local Government and Taxation of Towns Commission, Ireland, and Parliamentary Papers, 1871. An exchange between one of the Commissioners and a spokesman for the Kingstown Town Commissioners reads as follow:

> **Mr. Exham, QC**: Eleven years have passed since the passing of the Public Health Act and what has happened? Dr. O'Flaherty said that what Mr. Haliday said in his book was still in a great part true. He said there were numbers of places in the same condition still. No sewers, no ash pits, no privies, hovels over-crowded; in fact, places not fit for human habitation...
>
> **Dr. Roche**: Well, I think the worst part of it is the over-crowding – the people [take] in friends.
>
> **Mr. Exham**: Take in friends in places not fit for human habitation, which has not any sewer but the street, or privy or ashpit or no means of putting them in and where human filth is put in a bucket and thrown out at night in the public street.

The particular Haliday Dr. O'Flaherty was referring to was Charles Haliday who wrote the still-remembered *The Scandinavian Kingdom of Dublin*. Haliday was also the author of a scathing pamphlet decrying the conditions under which, by his calculations, a third of the inhabitants of Kingstown subsisted. His damning report is a reminder that behind the tourist's picture of stylish terraces, private parks where nursemaids tended well brought-up children and, yes, elegant yacht clubs there was a world of nightmarish squalor.

Such conditions were a danger to all. In 1866, four years before the laying of the foundation stone of what is now the National Yacht Club, cholera again struck the neighbourhood and 124 people died. By then it had been well-established that cholera had its roots in defective sanitation of which Kingstown's was a notorious example.

Dr. More Madden, who edited Haliday's pamphlet after his death, confirmed the contamination of Kingstown sanitation with samples of his own which he took from seven of the town's wells: 'five out of seven specimens which I examined contained organic matter and chlorine, which may be considered proof that the water is contaminated by sewage'.

Public water supply did not arrive at Kingstown until two months after the laying of the club's foundation stone. On 8 June 1870, in the presence of a large congregation of municipal worthies at the gates of Monkstown Castle, 'a hose was attached to the hydrant at the termination of the water main which had been carried beneath the high road nearly all the distance between Stillorgan reservoir and Monkstown ... from whence it will be conveyed by the Kingstown Commissioners into the township, which is in a deplorable state for the want of water'. On the water being turned on by Sir John Gray, 'it rose from the nozzle to a height of ninety feet in a dense column, when it distributed itself over the parched trees and along the arid and dusty roads.' (*Freeman's Journal*, 9 June 1870).

Up to then, noted the *Freeman* a year later, when supply had been carried into the Township, the inhabitants had to rely 'on semi-putrid rain water in musty and gangrene tanks, on the hard and unwholesome water from the local pumps of from what could be vended from Juggy's Well by the owners of donkey carts.'

Dr Jerome O'Flaherty died on 7 December 1888 and Dr Richard O'Flaherty on 15 February 1913.

23.

Jim Waller – Civil Engineer Extraordinaire

When looking back on lifetime full of achievement, Major James Hardress de Warrenne Waller, DSO, OBE, Master of Engineering, Master of Science, member of the Institution of Engineers, member of the Institution of Civil Engineers of Ireland (and also, on a more prosaic level, Rear-Commodore, National Yacht Club (1934-1939) used to say that his proudest achievement was membership of the Tasmanian Mineworkers Union.

This came about because on leaving school in Hobart, he took a job underground as a miner to gain practical experience to become a mining engineer. Throughout his life, he looked back on his two years in the mines as among his happiest and most interesting experiences. He formed a high opinion of the miners and they gave him his first understanding of the problems, thoughts and cares of the working man.

He was born near Hobart because it was to there that his father, George Arthur Waller, and his mother, Sarah, had emigrated from Ireland some years earlier. His father had been Chief Engineer and brewer in Guinness Brewery but, persuaded by Sarah (who had become very religious) that he could not in good conscience continue to brew an alcoholic beverage, he resigned from Guinness and set up a pottery business in Leitrim. This did not prosper – there were problems with Arigna coal – and they decided to emigrate to Tasmania, Embarking from Galway with his wife and four children, he brought their own cow to provide them with milk on the long journey.

In 1904 Jim came to Ireland to study civil engineering in what was then Queen's College, Galway. He studied for two years at Galway and after that another three years at the sister college in Cork, obtaining an MSC and an ME.

About this time he became fascinated by reinforced concrete which was still something of a novelty in building construction, and in 1910 he went to the US to see for himself what developments were taking place there. With this in mind, he took a job for six months supervising reinforced construction for the American Concrete-Steel Company, New Jersey.

Back in Ireland, he was made responsible for what he claimed to be the first reinforced concrete bridge in Ireland across an arm of the river at the college entrance. Persuading the college authorities to allow him to use this 'new-fangled' material was probably the most difficult part of the project. The fact that his views prevailed on that occasion, as on many others, was his ability to speak with simple logic, technical knowledge and persuasive conviction.

In 1911 he worked on the new reinforced concrete bridge across the Suir in the middle of Waterford town and then, in association with Alfred Delap, on another reinforced concrete bridge upstream from Wexford over the Slaney. From this came the partnership of Delap and Waller, the building services firm which remained in business until it was dissolved during the recent recession.

The 1914-18 war brought Jim Waller, serving with the Royal Engineers, to Gallipoli, Suvla Bay and the attack on Chocolate Hill. He was in the Balkan fighting and in the retreat from Serbia and saw service in Salonika. He rose to the rank of Major, and for his exploits and leadership was awarded the DSO and was three times mentioned in dispatches.

It was while at Salonica that he was sent to build a naval jetty at the Stavros, and from which later came his invention construction system now used extensively all over the world. With nothing to hand except large stocks of fencing wire, plenty of sand and green saplings, he made large baskets which he filled with rocks and then decked the rock-filled baskets with a concrete slab.

Faced then with the problem of using the fencing wire as re-inforcement for the concrete, his ingenious solution was to twist two strands together. He fastened two strands of wire between two trees and set a man in the middle to twist the strands together by means of a rod. The result was a bar of reinforcement of sufficient size and rigidity to use in the concrete. Years later this led to his invention and development of a system of reinforcement which he called 'coverbond'.

After this came No Frango. On one occasion, when inspecting the camouflage of tents on an outpost, Jim found a sergeant who, having no mud, the usual medium, had used a slurry of cement and water. Jim was impressed with the result. He entered the tent and removed the tent pole, to the consternation of the sergeant, but the tent remained standing.

Years later, he thought of that tent and what wonderful build-ing material could be made of cement mortar on canvas or hessian. From this came the No Frango ('I will not break') building material which ultimately, for a variety of reasons, was not a commercial success. Nevertheless a number of bungalows were built with it in Ireland as well as part of a factory. Examples of it still exist in a flat-roofed building in Loreto Avenue, Rialto.

Returning to Ireland in 1928, he set up – or resumed – practice with Alfred Delap. In 1934 employment was very severe in Ireland. State aid was small and, although various charities helped with cash in kind, many families were in deep distress. Jim and a friend, Paddy Somerville-Large, together with Hugh Delap, Alfred's son, collected a few enthusiasts and decided to do something practical to help.

They agreed that what the men needed above all was hope and self-confidence, and that the best way to get these things was not by providing them with money or goods, but with the means of get-ting for themselves the necessities of life. To this end, it was decided to establish some kind of centre. A derelict building in Mount Street

Dublin was acquired and renovated; workshops, a dining hall, recreation rooms, kitchens and other offices were constructed.

Jim was determined that it should not convey a gloomy picture or any suggestion of charity or rehabilitation. The most exclusive and self-regarding society in the city was, probably, the Kildare Street Club. So Jim suggested that the new venture should be called the 'Mount Street Club'. The name was adopted by unanimous acclaim and Dublin had gained another famous club.

Simultaneously with all this, Jim Waller was also Rear-Commodore of the National Yacht Club, arguing, among other things, for more rights and better facilities for women associates. As well as for the concrete slip on the eastern side of the club.

His numerous projects and his ingenious inventions are far too numerous to be discussed here but mention must be made of Ctesiphon construction, his building method based on the great arch of Ctesiphon which he had seen in the 1920s near Bagdad in Iraq. With this as a model, he set up a structure of temporary arched ribs of timber and covered them with an envelope of hessian fixed to the ribs. Plaster was then applied until the designed thickness was obtained. The hessian sagged between the ribs causing corrugations in the surface, which not only gave the shell a pleasing appearance but also the stiffness to resist lateral forces.

Many buildings were constructed using this system, including (in Ireland) Lockes's bonded warehouse at Kilbeggan and farm buildings at Grange, near Trim in County Meath.

In 1951 he developed cancer of the larynx. After the operation, which left him voiceless, he ignored the tube supplied in such cases to provide some degree of communication and by unremitting practice succeeded in producing reasonably intelligible speech. He died on 9 February 1968 from the effects of a stroke.

24.

Distant Shores

N.Y.C. CRUISING GROUP
6th Birthday Souvenir Menu
FRIDAY 10th OCTOBER, 1986.

On 22nd October, 1980, 9 members of the National sat in the bar and formed the Cruising Group. Six years later there are 50 Members and we are still growing, and still sitting in the bar!

(A) Cruising Group 1986

Above is an extract form the programme of National Yacht Club's cruising group which celebrated its sixth birthday in 1986. Memories may be hazy but some believe that the group dates back to the mid-seventies. Organisation was informal, cruises were arranged by ringing around, and depended on weather and who was availabille. The favoured cruising area was the Irish Sea but sometimes members of the group ventured to more distant shores. Nowadays Irish Sea sailing has been subsumed into ISORA (the Irish Sea Offshore Racing Association), one of whose pinciple organisers is Peter Ryan, National Yacht Club Commodore 2008-2011.

Member	Boat
Begley, Anita	*Eliminator*
Begley, Gordon & Sheila	*Some Tulip*
Blanchard, Jim	*Lyrad*
Byrne, John & Hilda	*Debonair*
Crotty, Martin	*Eliminator*
Dolan, Eamonn	*Isis Ruby*
Dwyer, Brian & Marie	*Elizabeth*
Fitzpatrick, Tony	*Nymphus*
Furlong, Dave & Anne	*Sante Fe*
Hanley, Theo & Louise	*Marie*
Jobling, Tony & Ann	*Tanda*
Leach, Jim	*Buccaneer*
Leahy, John	
Liddy, Myles	
Madigan, Alan & Margaret	*Panache*
McHenry, Cormac & Barbara	*Ring of Kerry*
McLysaght, Brian & Joan	*Esprit*
McNeaney, Barry	
McCabe, Joe & Mary	*Einmara*
McConnell, Winder	
Nolan, Gerry	*Buccaneer*
O'Donovan, Ronnie	*Setanta*
O'Kelly, Liam & Marjorie	*Poseidon*
O'Regan, Louise	*Stragill*
O'Rourke, Cathal & Jo	*Seajay*
Roy, John & Joan	*Pegeen*
Ryan, Frank	*Aracaty*
Sheil, Leonard & Hazel	*Gay Gannett*
Thompson, Laurie	*Shindilla*
Totterdell, Eddie & Bridie	*Avanti*
Williams, George	*Adastra*

(b) From the Aegean to the South Seas

Conor O'Regan (NYC Hon. Treasurer 2016-2020) recalls a memorable circumnavigation.

In 2002 we bought a Rival 38, *Pamina* which was located in Rome. Henrietta had no sailing experience at that time, so our first cruise was along the Italian coast from Rome south to the Pontine Islands and then to the Bay of Naples and back. The following year we set off on a cruise around the Mediterranean with a view to a possible North Atlantic circuit to extend our season if things went well. At several points in the early days of sailing, issues with the engine, rigging and wiring needed attention, but we addressed them and, as time went on, *Pamina* became more and more reliable.

After sailing as far east as Aegina in the Aegean, we set our sights westward and made quick progress back to the Ionian and then onwards to Malta, Sardinia, the Balearics and Gibraltar. We crossed from Gibraltar to the Canaries where, after a month's preparation,

Henrietta and Conor O'Regan

Pamina

we set sail for St Lucia in November 2003. We were fortunate that my father Brendan joined us for the transatlantic as it meant a lighter night watch rota for the three of us. Our first transatlantic proved to be a slow, but enjoyable and uneventful, 26 day crossing in generally light winds.

While I had given some attention to heavy weather sail plans, not enough thought had been given to light winds. During the slower days, I started thinking about how to optimise the sail plan and improve on our goose-wing jib/main combination which was slow and very rolly.

In the Caribbean, having spoken to several skippers who had made quicker passages, I decided that a poled-out twin-jib set-up would work well for us. As we only had one slot in the foil, I instructed a sailmaker to make twin-jibs stitched to a single bolt-rope. It was an innovation that neither the sailmaker nor myself had come across previously. As it was on the furler we could reduce or increase sail area quickly. Many year later, Elstrom would bring such a sail to market as a revolutionary innovation.

The 'twins' as we called them transformed our tradewind sailing: our daily average was now 150 nautical miles where previously that mileage would have been an exceptionally fast day. Having enjoyed the Atlantic and the Caribbean, we decided to continue sailing instead of returning to Europe. In March 2004, we set off from Grenada to Panama, transited through the Panama Canal and sailed onwards to the Galapagos, the Marquesas and Society Islands. In the Marquesas, we were joined by Brendan once more – he had travelled by air/road for 48 hours, via Paris, LA and Tahiti and finally down a treacherous dirt mountain pass to find us at anchor in Nuku Hiva.

Together the three of us spent several wonderful weeks exploring French Polynesia and the Tuamotus, learning how to navigate coral atolls with unreliable charts and a dash of courage. As before, Brendan was the best crew and brought us delightful company, news and Christmas cake from Louise. After dropping Brendan in Tahiti where we enjoyed some days of 'city comforts' and well stocked chandleries, Brendan left and we continued to sail on through Moorea, Raiatea, Bora Bora, the Cook Islands and Niue. We completed that season with a final leg from Tonga to New Zealand.

In March 2005 we left *Pamina* in Whangarai, North Island, and returned to Europe to work for about a year. On our return to New Zealand in 2006, we spent several weeks preparing and upgrading the boat before finally sailing north to Vanuatu in early July, the 'depths' of the New Zealand winter. We left Vanuatu with a

Pamina's Twin Jibs

plan to make landfall in Australia. We enjoyed being back on board and loved the freedom of offshore cruising, so instead of calling into Australia as originally planned, we sailed past all of mainland Australia without a stop which took 27 days, arriving after 4,000 nautical miles at Christmas Island. The onward trip would take us to Cocos Keeling, Chagos, Madagascar and along the wild South African coast.

We arrived in Richard's Bay in some of the worst conditions we had experienced to date and the welcome party in the local restaurant turned from lunch to dinner, as we were joined by other sailors who had come through the storm. We spent several months exploring South Africa from our base in Durban Marina. Brendan joined us for a few weeks to sail with us around the Horn of Africa and into Cape Town.

From Cape Town, we then sailed to St Helena and onward for our second Atlantic crossing. We completed our circumnavigation with a 30-day sail from St Helena to Grenada in March 2007. Our third and final Atlantic crossing in this cruise was from Antigua to Horta, and finally we sailed to Glandore where we made our first landfall in Europe in over three years. From Glandore, we leisurely picked our way up the Irish coast in beautiful weather until we eventually arrived in Dún Laoghaire in July 2007, where we have been based ever since. It was a fantastic cruise, one which we enjoyed immensely.

We never regret our decision to keep sailing westwards from Greece. What started as a Mediterranean cruise turned into an Atlantic crossing and then a circumnavigation plus two Atlantic crossings.

Pamina's Routes

25.

The Maguire Model Yacht Collection

W illiam Arthur Maguire, Commodore of the National Yacht Club, 1979-1983, was a man of many parts. Architect, painter, gardiner, water colourist, administrator, he tackled each role with energy, a great clarity of mind and a discriminating intelligence. He could have been a distinguished lawyer like his father, Supreme Court Justice Martin Maguire, because, besides intelligence, he had great persuasive powers and could command a room on tumultous occasions. But architecture was his vocation and he graduated with first class honours from UCD in 1946.

Admitted to the Royal Institute of the Architects of Ireland in 1946, he returned later to lecture at UCD in its school of architecture. He was elected President of the RIAI in 1971. Among the projects his architectural practice was associated with was the restoration of the King's Inns and Registry of Deeds, a Gandon-designed structure, requiring rebuilding of exposed granite and portland stone, and the internal refurbishment of the building.

He had considerable administrative and managerial gifts. He became chairman in 1972 of the National College of Art an Design after a period of student unruliness and staff unrest. Willie Maguire played a key role in resolving the crisis, leading towards degrees, better salary scales and the move to new premises away from its its cramped location between Dáil Éireann and the National Library. Co-opted to the Board of the Irish Permanent Building Society in 1978, he served as director for nine years. His skills as a negotia-

Maguire Model Yacht Collection

tor were much appreciated when, as arbitrator, he helped resolve a number of complicated building contract disputes.

He took up sailing in 1953 and it became a ruling passion for the next fifty years. He first sailed on the Dublin Bay Twenty One Footer, *Garvogue*, which belonged to his architectural colleague, A. A. Murphy, and then moved to *Naneen* with his friend, Michael O'Herlihy. On the death of Frank Lemass in 1974 he acquired the latter's Dublin Bay Twenty Four Footer *Fenestra*, which he raced regularly in Dublin Bay until 2002.

Willie Maguire was of a generation of architects that learned the model-maker's skills so that their projects could be displayed *in parvo* to clients. With time on his hands, he tuned to making scale models of traditional Dublin Bay yachts. *Naneen* is among them, and *Fenestra*, and *Punctilio* a famous Twenty Five Footer in her day, as well as a J.B. Kearney Mermaid, a Seventeen Footer, and a James A. Doyle Colleen. It was all meticulously well done and thoroughly researched, each model taking over a year to complete.

When he died in February 2007, his widow, Ailbhe, presented the collection of Willie's yacht models to the National Yacht Club. It is displayed in a fine Peter Crowley-designed cabinet on the club's lower ground floor. Nowadays, with racing in Dublin Bay dominated by mass-produced GRP craft, Willie Maguire's collection is a magnificent tribute to the skills of the boat-builders of a by-gone age, and a splendid record of the wooden boats that generations of members sailed out of the National Yacht Club.

26.

Brendan the Navigator and the Dublin Bay Sailing Club 21 Footers

Foxrock parishioners attending services at the Church of Perpetual Succour in Foxrock might sometimes cast a glance at the stained glass window three-quarters of the way up the aisle, on the wall on the right-hand side. It's in honour of St Brendan the Navigator and was presented to Foxrock parish by Ken and Muriel Ryan in memory of Frank and Maureen Ryan. Frank died in 1988 and Maureen in 2001.

Representations of boats are to be expected in such a work but (looking closer) visitors might be intrigued by the particlar variety of boat here represented – a fleet of Dublin Bay 21 Footers in their original gaff-rig, with top-sails aloft; the profiles of the two boats in the foreground are nondescript but the names of the boats the artist had in mind are clearly shown, *Estelle* and *Naneen* (*Naneen* and the other Twenty Ones suffered grievously during the storm of 1985 but is scheduled to reappear in a new guise in Dublin Bay in 2020, thanks to the dedicated work of Hal Sisk and Fionán de Barra).

About the identity of the bald-headed helmsan of *Estelle* there can be no doubt. It's that of Frank Ryan, at one time head of Abbey Stained Glass Studios, who sailed in various boats in Dublin Bay from about 1944. A scaled-down copy was produced at the same time as the window, and his son, Ken, presented it to the National Yacht Club where it was erected on the lower

IN MEMORY OF
FRANK AND MAUREEN RYAN.
DIED 1988 AND 2001.
ERECTED BY MURIEL AND KEN RYAN.

St Brendan the Navigator

ground floor near the door to the forecourt. The light there is particularly subdued, very suitable it was thought, for the display of a
stained glass work. The artist was Kevin Kelly who died aged 92 in
2019.

Estelle was one of the several boats sailed by Frank Ryan and his
partners, John McKinney, Niall Meagher (father of Niall Meagher,
Chairman of the 2019 Flying 15 Worlds event, hosted by the club)
and Billy Cotter. (The latter was the father of Michael Cotter, the
Dragon sailor and owner of the classic *Halloween*.) They had adven-
turous times afloat.

During the war years, when Frank lived on the North Side – he
was possibly a member of Clontarf YBC at the time – he had a die-
sel motor boat which he and his friend, the artist Fergus O'Farrell,
tried to start, late one night, on Dollymount strand. This was war
time and engines in boats were forbidden. The alarm was raised,

an invasion was feared and in no time they were surrounded by forces of the State. They were lucky not to have to spend the rest of the night under lock and key. Instead, they were spoken to most severely. There was also some misadventures involving a Wayfarer – or a boat called *Wayfarer* – which somehow or other got mislaid on the way up the coast from Wexford.

Estelle, on one occasion, set sail for the Isle of Man, helmed by the late Willie Earley, a member of the ecclesiastical art family. Willie was a better stained glass artist than he was navigator, and weather, winds and currents being adverse, *Estelle* and crew ended up on the coast of County Down near Bangor. Nerys, Ken's sister, then a child, remembers the Ryan house filled with wet sails and damp sailing clothes at the time. (*Estelle* had a number of owners after that, including Paul Winkelmann and Albert Foley, who was given her by the class on condition he restored her, after she had sunk in Seapoint Bay.)

Then there was *Tryphena*, a 38 foot, 10 ton sloop designed by Laurent Giles & Partners, which, on the evening of one of the Wicklow Regattas – much frequented at the time by Dublin Bay sailors – went on fire. Michael Cotter recalls that when he was trying to light a stove in the cabin, he was unaware that fuel from the engine had leaked out onto the floor. The ensuing fire was brought under control with the help of crews of adjoining boats. An American crewman, said to be a member of the New York fire brigade, was not much help. He fell over board and had to be rescued during all the excitement.

The travails of their next boat, *Aracaty III*, could not be laid at anyone else's door. It broke loose during the 1986 storm and went aground in the inner Coal Harbour, lying, it is remembered, with a gaping hole in her side.

The quartet's final boat was *Zubenubi*. Nothing to record there except to recall that all of the Ryan family's cats were named after their boats. Somebody remembers seeing in the local vet's office a cat in a cage bearing the identifcation label, 'Zubenubi Ryan'.

Addenda

Flag & Honorary Officers (1902-1968)

Comm.	Vice Comm.	Rear Comm.	Hon. Secretary	Hon. Treasurer
			M. Barrington (1902)	Mr. T.W. Berry (1902)
			D.M. Turner (1903)	B.S. Mara (1910)
			W.N. Stewart (1904)	H. Moffitt (1911)
			Dr. O'Flaherty (1908)	W.B. Stuart (1913)
			H. Moffitt (1913)	J. Johnston (1918)
			John Lloyd (1918)	Capt. H. Macraith (1928)
			J.S. McIntyre (1931)	J. Lloyd (1931)
Earl of Pembroke (1921)	G.A. Newsom (1921)	Henry Falkiner (1921)	Henry Baxter (1932)	W. Trevor Roper (1939)
Earl of Granard (1931)	P.J .Lawrence (1931)	Dr. C.B. Scott (1924)	Sealy Jeffares (1933)	J.J. Ryan (1942)
Earlof Granard resignd 1941	Master O'Hanlon (1933)	Master O'Hanlon (1932)	Louis Stiven (1940)	A. McMurray (1944)
T.J. Hamilton (1942)	T.J. Hamilton (1934)	Dr.C.B. Scott (1933)	R.B. Clark (1941)	P. McDermott (1945)

P.M. Purcell (1944)	J.B.. Kearney (1942)	Major J.H.Waller (1934)	T.R. Stewart (1944)	J.J. O'Leary (1950)
J.J. O'Leary (1946)	J.J. Macken (1952)	Harry Peard (1939)	D.L. Gibson (1946)	Dr.A Delaney (1951)
A.A. Murphy (1950)	R.A. Kidney (1960)	J. Spiro (1942)	D.M. Douglas 1963	J.R. Clark 1952
J.J. O'Leary (1955)	H. Hardy (1963)	R. Disney Gray (1944)	C.A. Lavery (1968)	F.B. Farley (1961)
Frank Lemass (1960)	R.A. Kidney (1964)	F.W .Brownlee (1952)		R.A. Kidney (1963)
J.C. McConnell (1965)	J.J. Walker (1965)	P. McGloughlin (1956)		F.B. Farley (1964)
	P.J. Johnston (1967)	R.A. Kidney (1958)		W. Miley (1966)
		Herbert Hardy (1960)		
		J.C. McConnell (1963)		
		P.J. Johnston (1965)		
		D. McGloughlin (1967)		

Commodores, 1969-2019

1969 Paul Johnston

1972 Liam Boyd

1974 Franz Winkelmann

1976 Philip Brown

1979 William Maguire

1983 Fred Cooney

1987 John Byrne

1988 Malachi Muldoon

1991 Brian Barry

1994 Michael Horgan

1997 Barry McNeaney

2000 Ida Kiernan

2002 Chris Moore

2005 Con Murphy

2008 Peter Ryan

2011 Paul Barrington

2014 Larry Power

2017 Ronan Beirne

2019 Martin McCarthy

Chronology

- 1869 – Inaugural meeting Kingstown Royal Harbour Boat Club (26th November).

- 1870 – Invitation to builders to tender (foundation, basement and stores, 15th February)

- 1870 – Laying of foundation stone by the Earl of Longford (20th April).

- 1871 – Issue of first debenture for £2,000 (26th May).

- 1871 – Open for reception of members (1st June).

- 1874 – Earl of Longford elected President of the Club.

- 1880 – Liquidation of Club (3rd December).

- 1881 – Sold at auction to a syndicate for £1250 (21st May).

- 1881 – Syndicate manages premises as a proprietary club (July).

- 1882 – First yacht race of Kingstown Yacht club (17th June).

- 1883 – Registration of club as Kingstown Yacht Club Ltd (3rd February).

- 1887 – Liquidation of Kingstown Yacht Club Ltd (3rd March 1887).

- 1887 – Purchase of Club by Charles Barrington (12th July). Sanctioned by Master of Rolls.

- 1887 – Assignment of assets to Charles Barrington, Absolute Club (21st December).

- 1901 – Death of Charles Barrington (20th April).

- 1901 – Transfer of club to trustees of Edward Yacht Club (28th October).

- 1921 – Earl of Pembroke elected Commodore (29th October).

- 1931 – Club re-named National Yacht Club (7th March).

- 1931 – Ceremonial re-naming of club and declaration of Earl of Granard as Commodore (18th July).

- 1932 – Earl of Grenard confirmed as Commodore (AGM, 18th June 1932).

- 1941 – Resignation of the Earl of Granard as Commodore. Succeeded by T.J. Hamilton (13 June 1942).

- 1975 – Fire and clubhouse reconstruction.

- 1984 – Fire and clubhouse reconstruction.

- 1998/9 – Forecourt extension.

- 2004/7 – Clubhouse enhancement.

Insignia of the National Yacht Club

The National Yacht Club has long been in the unique position of being permitted by the Chief Herald to use the State Harp (the Brian Boru Harp) in silver as an emblem. The official State emblem is a gold harp. No other yacht club has this distinction. Other clubs which use the harp use a variety of different designs.

FLAGS OF THE
NATIONAL YACHT CLUB

Burgee

37.1 Burgee: *triangular, blue and white quartered, red St George's Cross, blue to hoist.*

The Club burgee should only be flown from the masthead.

Club Ensign

37.2 Club Ensign: *The Club ensign shall be the field azure, in the first quarter the national tricolour of green, white and orange; in the centre of the fourth quarter a four stringed harp argent, and shall be subject to regulations imposed upon the Club by the Department of the Marine.*

The ensign may only be worn aboard a vessel owned by the holder of a warrant which must be obtained from the Club, such a warrant must be on board the vessel when the ensign is worn. The National Ensign must be flown from the stern of a vessel or from the masthead of the mizen mast. The National Yacht Club is privileged to be the only Club with permission to include the State Harp in its ensign.

Commodore

37.3 Commodore: *Club burgee in the form of a broad pennant with swallow tail.*

Vice Commodore

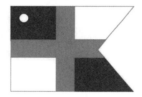

37.4 Vice-Commodore: *Club burgee in the form of a broad pennant with swallow tail with the addition of a white ball in the blue quarter to the hoist.*

Rear Commodore

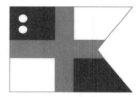

37.5 Rear Commodore: *Club burgee in the form of a broad pennant swallow tail with the addition of two white balls in the blue quarter to the hoist.*

37.6 Past Commodore,
37.6 Past Vice-Commodore
and
37.6 Past Rear Commodore
shall be identical to the flag of the respective officers, but with a vertical stripe, argent, upon the hoist.

House Flag

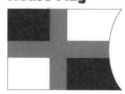

The House Flag *shall be rectangular and of the same colour and design as the Burgee, but with a shallow or obtuse swallow tailed.*

The House Flag shall be flown by a member's yacht from the starboard spreader where the mast head is not available for a club burgee. When visiting another country and flying the house flag, the courtesy flag must be flown from the superior higher position with the house flag immediately underneath. Other flags should be flown under the house flag.

Trans-Atlantic Pennant

The Trans-Atlantic Pennant *shall be the same colour and design as the burgee, but shall be some 60" long and 8" wide at the hoist.*

This pennant shall be awarded by the Flag Officers of the Club to a Full Member who has completed a Trans-Atlantic crossing.

Members are requested to adhere to the correct protocol with flying the Club flags.
Ronan Beirne, Rear Commodore

NYC Staff Sesquicentennial Year 2020

Club Manager, Tim O'Brien (2011-2020)

Tim has been the National Yacht Club's Manager since 2011, succeeding. Padraic Ó Conghaile in April of that year. A native of Stoneyford, County Kilkenny, he went to school at the Cistercian College, Roscrea and has a diploma in Business Studies and Marketing from Carlow IT.

Tim now lives in Athboy, County Meath with his wife Julie, and their four children, Sally, Connor, Timmy and Bobby. He has spent most of his working life in County Meath where he has been Vice-Chairman of Meath Tourism and Co-Founder of the Meath Good Food Circle. He worked for the O'Callaghan Hotel Group as Banqueting Manager between 1990 and 1993. In 1994 he commissioned and opened the Old Darnley Lodge and ran it as General Manager for six years. The Old Darnley Lodge had a huge wedding business of over 150 weddings a year a as well as Buck Mulligan's Night Club, being the largest club venue in the north-east with a capacity for over 2,000 patrons. In 1999 he opened Franzini O'Brien's Restaurant in Trim, in 2003 O'Brien's Good Food and Drink House, Navan and in 2005 the Russell Restaurant, Navan. He has been Consultative Council member of the Food Safety Authority of Ireland since 2008.

Sailing Manager, Olivier Prouvier

Olivier was born at Valenciennes near the Belgian border. He qualified as State Civil Engineer at one of France's 'Grandes écoles' and learned to sail while a student. He came to Ireland as Commercial Attaché to the French Embassy as part of his conscription (military service). This appointment was extended by another six years.

Olivier then worked for the Institute of European Affairs and afterwards set up tech companies (multi-media/mobile content/web streaming). In 2006 he started in the NYC as Sailing Manager. He ran the DMYC Frostbite series for 18 years and served as a volunteer on the committee boat for four years before that. He has raced with DBSC since 1995. He is married to Caríosa Power, an active dinghy sailor and a one-time dinghy class captain.

Cormac Healy, *Chef de Cuisine*

Cormac Healy has been the National Yacht Club's *Chef de Cuisine* for twenty-six years. His family roots go back many generations in Dún Laoghaire and the South County Dublin area; his parents owned *Violet Hill*, Ballybrack, once the property of the Captain Peacocke mentioned earlier (See Chapter 6).

Cormac's formative years in catering were spent in Boston in the US where he worked in prestigious undertakings such as the Park Plaza , a Boston landmark, and the Bay Tower Rooms in the 60 States Street skyscraper, a location much favoured by the Boston political establishment. He later worked in the Michelin-starred Portman International in London, and in Ireland, White's on the Green, Café Clara, Wright's Brasserie and, locally, Digby's. Cormac's knowledge of world cuisine has enabled him to furnish, on demand, an eclectic range of international dishes.

Wayne Anthony, Head Boatman

Wayne has been with the National Yacht Club since March 2007. Born in Capetown, he joined the South African Navy at an early age, qualifying as a sonar operator in SA's Mines Counter Measures Section. He was seven years at sea. NYC boatowners who marvel at Wayne's boat handling skills – which include miraculously shinning up a mast unaided by any climibng gear – should know that he is a highly qualified professional yachtsman. Like other navies, the SA navy gives priority to yachting as an approved sport for its personnel and Wayne had the good fortune to spend seven years on the SA Navy sailing team, finishing as an instructor in seamanship and and sail training.

Robert Malcolmson, Bar Manager

Robert first started in the National Yacht Club in 1997 having arrived in Ireland with his fiancé after a successful two years managing a 17th century village green pub just outside Lewes. He was born in Hertfordshire, the youngest of eight, the year before England won the World Cup. The family moved to West Sussex in the early 1970s and he enjoyed a childhood exploring the South Downs. He did not intend to stay long in the NYC bar but found the waterfront and the Irish mode of life an invigorating mix.

Oonagh Deegan, Office Manager

Oonagh has worked in the NYC since March 2009. After graduating from Rockford Manor secondary school, and while studying childcare, she took up part-time employment with Penneys in Dún Laoghaire. After college an opportunity arose in Penneys head office in the post room. Once there she worked her way up to the Operations Department and eventually the Visual Merchandising Department. In 2001, after 11 years with the company, she decided it was time to move on and took an Office Manager position with the Carpet Showrooms based in Bray. She was happily employed there until 2007 when she moved to the newly refurbished Royal Marine Hotel as PA to the General Manager. After the downturn in 2009 and redundancy from the hotel, Padraic ÓConghaile hired her as a receptionist in the NYC. Originally from Glenageary, she now lives with her husband Pat and their son Paddy in Dún Laoghaire.

Manager Tim O'Brien and Catering Staff, January 2020

Bibliography

Archer, Stella and Peter Pearson, *Royal St. George Yacht Club: A History* (1987) Dublin: City Office Ltd.

Bender, Mike, *A New History of Yachting* (2017) Suffolk, UK: Boydell and Brewer

Boylan, Henry, *White Sails Crowding: A History of the Royal Irish Yacht Club* (1994), Dublin: A&A Farmar

Cosgrave, E. McDowel, *Dublin and County Dublin in the 20th Century* (1908) N.T. Pike & Co.

Costelloe, Capt. Con (Ed.), *An Cosantóir*, Magazine of the Irish Defence Forces (April 1973)

Delany, Vincent, *International 12 Foot Dinghies in Ireland* (2018) private publication

Dictionary of Irish Architects

Dictionary of Irish Biography (Royal Irish Academy)

Hamilton, Mary, *Green and Gold* (1948) London: Allan Windgate

Harmon, Maurice, *Sean O'Faolain: A Life* (1994) London: Constable

Irish Builder (1869-1871)

Irish Field

Irish Newspaper Archive (National Library of Ireland)

Laffan, Moira, *The Barringtons of Glendruid* (1990) Dublin: Foxrock Local History Club

Lawlor, Col. A.T., Ed., *Irish Maritime Survey* (1945), Dublin: Parkside Press

Lloyds Yacht Register

McNally, Errol, Ed., *Irish Yachting* (1946) Dublin: Parkside Press

Minute Books, Dublin Bay Sailing Club

Minute Books, Edward Yacht Club (1902-1931)

Minute Books, National Yacht Club (1931-1968)

Minutes Books, Royal St. George Yacht Club

Minutes, Royal Irish Yacht Club

National Archives of Ireland

Nixon, W.M. *Howth: A Centenary of Sailing* (1995) Howth: Howth Yacht Club

O'Sullivan, Donal J., *The Spice of Life* (1948) Dublin: Brown and Nolan

Pakenham, Valerie, *Maria Edgeworth's Letters from Ireland* (2018), Dublin: Lilliput.

Parliamentary Papers (Second report of the Royal Sanitary Commission 1871.Vol.XXXV)

Pearson, Peter, *Dún Laoghaire–Kingstown* (1981) Dublin: O'Brien Press

Registry of Deeds

Simington, Thomas A., *Reminiscences of Thomas A. Simington*, a private memoir (no date) (with a biography of James Hardress de Warrenne Waller D.S.O., O.B.E. by Andrew Ross).

Thoms Directory

Yachting World (1894)

Photo Credits

Donal O'Sullivan and the National Yacht Club are grateful to all who supplied photographs to illustrate this work. Because of the Covid 19 shutdown, the original source and copyright of a small number of the photos have been difficult to establish. If some mis-attribution has ocuured, our apologies to those concerned. We will endeavour to correct any errors in subsequent editions.

Pages viii-ix – Photo thanks to representatives of the late Pat Whelan

Page xii – Source unknown

Page 5 – DBSC archives

Page 12 – Photo courtesy of Dún Laoghaire Borough Historical Society

Page 17 – Carlow Co.Council library service

Page 19 – National Archives

Page 22 – NYC archives

Page 25 – Courtesy of Tom Conlon

Page 30 – Lawrence Collecton. Image Courtesy of the National Library of Ireland

Page 37 – Photo by author

Page 39 – Photo by author

Page 41 – Photo of portrait of Charles Barrington by Sir Thomas Jones, PRHA, courtesy Ron Barrington

Page 50 – Portrait by Dermod O'Brien, PRHA, courtesy Hugh Lane Gallery

Page 51 – Lawrence collection, Image Courtesy of the National Library of Ireland

Page 52 – Courtesy of Thomas Ryan, PRHA

Page 65 – Hargrave Collecton, Image Courtesy of the National Library of Ireland

Page 70 – NYC Collection

Page 75 – Courtesy *Irish Independent*

Page 80 – Photo by Ronan Beirne

Page 83 – Wikipedia

Page 88 – Photo Tom Hudson

Page 98 – Photo Ronan Beirne

Page 102 – Portrait by Nano Reid, NYC collection

Page 104 – Irish Photo Archive (Lensmen)

Page115 – Photo by author

Page 116 – Photo by Beken

Page 117 – Photo courtesy *The Irish Times*

Page 127 – Justin Merrigan collection

Page 128 – Extract RTÉ programme Broadsheet

Page 129 – DBSC archives (Jack Kennedy)

Page 129 – Photo of Jack Brennan by author

Page 137 – Photo courtesy Lucy Burke

Page 138 – Photo by author

Page 139 – Exract, RTÉ programme Broadsheet

Page 141 – Photo Michael Chester

Page 144 – Photo by author

Page 146 – Photo by author

Page 147 – Photo courtesy Barbara McHenry

Page 148 – Photos by author

Page 150 – Photo by author

Page 151 – Photo by Brian Keane

Page 152 – DBSC archives

Page 155 – Source unknown (RNLI fund-raising event)

Page 158 – Photo courtesy David Cooney

Page 159 – Photo courtesy F. De Barra

Page 162 – Photo by F. De Barra

Page 171 – Photo by author

Page 174 – Photo by author

Page 175 – Photo courtesy Richard Hooper

Pages 178-179 – Photos courtesy Michael Rothschild

Page 180 – Photo by author

Page 183 – Photo by author

Page 184 – Photo by author

Pages 195, 196, 198, 199 – Photos courtesy C. O'Regan

Page 201 – Photo by author

Page 204 – Photo by author

Page 211 – Photo courtesy K. Slattery

Pages 213-215 – Photos by author

Page 216 – Photo of O. Deegan

Page 217 – NYC collection

Index